CONTENTS

PREFACE

By BRENDAN FOSTER MBE

I was first drawn to athletics by the magic of the Olympics when, as a twelve-year-old schoolboy, I watched the television pictures of master runners like Herb Elliott and Abebe Bikila striking gold in the 1960 Games in Rome. The Olympics, the greatest sports show on earth, have had a hold on me ever since, and in this book I have selected the outstanding heroes from all sports who have illuminated the Olympic arena with their performances. I have also tried to predict the likely heroes of the 1984 Olympic track and field championships in Los Angeles, but when judging my selections I hope you will bear in mind that I had to get my thoughts down on paper long before the competitors were unveiling their Olympic-year form.

The 'Foster's Favourites' section is all about *opinion* while Part Two of the book is devoted to *fact* about some of the great Olympic heroes of the past. I was given considerable help in drawing all the facts and figures together by sportswriter Norman Giller, and I could not have been nearly as specific and authoritative without continual reference to the following publications:
The Olympic Games (edited by Lord Killanin and John Rodda, 1980); *Encyclopaedia of the Olympic Games* (Erich Kamper, 1972); *The Olympic Games Book* (Harold Abrahams, 1956); *The Guinness Book of Olympic Records* (edited by Norris McWhirter); various articles and statistics in *Athletics Weekly* (edited by Mel Watman) and in the fine American publication *Track and Field News*.

From the age of twelve, I dreamt of becoming an Olympic hero. I managed fifth place in the 1500 metres final in Munich in 1972, and ran myself into the ground for a bronze medal behind the modern 'Flying Finn' Lasse Viren in the 10,000 metres final in Montreal four years later. In Moscow I was betrayed by my legs on the last lap of the 10,000 metres and struggled home in 11th place. Even though I still have the honour of holding the Olympic record for 5000 metres, I didn't make it to hero status. I achieved only pygmy performances compared with the giants of Olympic history who are featured in Part Two. It is to these heroes that I dedicate this book on behalf of all the twelve-year-olds who have been set dreaming by their performances.

The Los Angeles Memorial Stadium: ready and waiting for the start of the 1984 Games

PART ONE

FOSTER'S FAVOURITES

In alphabetical order, the athletes Brendan Foster expects to emerge as the gold-striking heroes of Los Angeles 1984

Gennady Avdeyenko: high hopes in LA

GENNADY AVDEYENKO (USSR)

Event: Men's high jump
Olympic record: 2.36m Gerd Wessig (GDR) 1980

Fact file:
Born November 4 1963
Ht 6 ft 7 in. Wt 176 lb
World champion 1983
Personal best: 2.32 metres, 1983

BRENDAN FOSTER: Gennady Avdeyenko was taken to the 1983 world championships in Helsinki as Russian third string purely for the experience, and to prepare him for major competitions later in his career. He shocked everybody (including himself) by winning the world title. Among those left looking up to him were current world record holder Zhu Jian Hua, of China, ex-world record holders Jacek Wszola from Poland (the 1976 Olympic champion), Dietmar Mogenburg of West Germany (the 1982 European champion) and American Dwight Stones. It was American third string Tyke Peacock, the 1981 World Cup winner, who gave Avdeyenko the hardest battle for the championship. The nineteen-year-old Soviet soldier from Odessa showed incredible control and composure in his first major championship and pipped Peacock on a countback to failures after they had both cleared a personal best height of 2.32 metres. It was his coolness in one of the most keenly contested high-jump competitions of all time that convinced me that Avdeyenko has the all-important temperament to go with his obvious talent. He can only get better and it will be fascinating to see if he can again come out on top against the springheeled Zhu Jian Hua, who will be attempting to win China's first ever Olympic athletics gold medal.

UDO BEYER (East Germany)

Event: Men's shot
Olympic record: 21.35m Vladimir Kiselyev (USSR), 1980

Fact file:
Born August 9 1955
Ht 6 ft 5 in. Wt 275 lb
Olympic champion 1976, European champion 1978 and 1982
World Cup winner 1977 and 1979
Set world shot record of 22.22 metres in 1983

BRENDAN FOSTER: Beyer squeezed into the 1976 Olympics as a twenty-year-old shot specialist who was virtually untried in the international arena. All of us in the British team were rooting for big Geoff Capes, but along with the favourites — Russian Aleksandr Baryshnikov and Americans Al Feuerbach and George Woods — he failed to produce his peak power when it really mattered. Beyer, with nothing to lose, was the most relaxed man in the final, where nerves were really jangling. Because they are such big, fearsome-looking men there is a tendency to think they don't suffer from nerves but butterflies can attack their stomachs just as much as they do the track competitors. Beyer later described some of his rivals as being 'almost hysterical and crazy with nerves.' He kept his cool and won with a putt of just over 69 feet. Beyer, who can also throw a mean hammer, has since been the dominant force in the shot but injury prevented him retaining the Olympic title in Moscow and he was again handicapped by injury in the world championships in Helsinki when Poland's Edward Sarul emerged as a surprising champion. If Beyer is at anything like his top form in Los Angeles he should regain the Olympic crown. The United States have three formidable competitors in Dave Laut, Mike Lehmann and Kevin Akins and Beyer can also expect tough opposition from his countryman Ulf Timmermann. It's difficult to make accurate predictions about any of the throwing events because of the scandal of drug abuse. There is going to be a stricter than ever medical check in LA to try to curb the use of steroids that illegally increase weight and strength. This could lead to a lot of below-par performances in Los Angeles by athletes forced to abandon their drug-taking routine.

SERGEY BUBKA (USSR)

Event: Men's pole vault
Olympic record: 5.78m Wladyslaw Kozakiewicz (POL) 1980

Fact file:
Born December 4 1963
Ht 5ft 10¾in. Wt 150 lb
World champion 1983
Personal best: 5.70 metres, 1983 (5.82m indoors, 1984)

BRENDAN FOSTER: Sergey Bubka impressed everyone with his competitive steel in the 1983 world championships in Helsinki when he showed a maturity beyond his years, keeping his nerve and his concentration while all around him more experienced vaulters were losing their composure. He and high-jumper Gennady Avdeyenko are spearheading a new wave of Russian superathletes, and at twenty Bubka could emerge as one of the youngest track and field champions in LA. Vaulters seem to hunt in pairs. Russia have Bubka and Konstantin Volkov, first and second in Helsinki, at the top of their class. The United States will be looking to Jeff Buckingham and indoor king Billy Olson to put America back on the gold standard in an event that they used to dominate. France have two exceptional challengers in current world record holder Thierry Vigneron (5.83m) and the man from whom he took the record, Pierre Quinon, while the Poles, fittingly, have a pair of potential medallists in defending champion Wladyslaw Kozakiewicz and the veteran Tadeusz Slusarski. The competition is so fierce that the winner seems certain to be taking his final vault under floodlight in the Los Angeles Coliseum at the climax of an event that will hold the attention of spectators for hours.

IMRICH BUGAR (Czechoslovakia)

Event: Men's discus
Olympic record: 68.28m Mac Wilkins (USA) 1976

Fact file:
Born April 14 1955
Ht 6 ft 5 in. Wt 264 lb
Olympic silver medallist 1980, European champion 1982
World champion 1983
Personal best: 70.72m

BRENDAN FOSTER: Bugar is a positive competitor who always gets himself right — both physically and mentally — for the major championships. Watch him in his first two visits to the throwing circle because that is when he will be going all out to get a psychological advantage over his rivals. He said after his victory in the 1983 world championships: 'I always try to produce my best form at the very beginning of the final competition because this is when you can make a big impression on the rest of the competitors.' He won the world title in Helsinki with his second throw, and will be looking to make the same early impact in Los Angeles, when among his rivals for the gold medal will be Cuban Luis Delis, vastly experienced Americans Ben Plucknett, John Powell and 1976 Olympic champion Mac Wilkins and Bugar's countryman Geza Valent. Russian Yuriy Dumchev remains an unknown quantity. He produced an 'out of the blue' world record of 71.86 metres in 1983, but was a complete flop in Helsinki in his first competition outside the USSR.

Opposite
Udo Beyer: the 'Big Shot' of athletics

Sergey Bubka: a lot of talent in the vault

Opposite
Imrich Bugar: man with the golden arm

14

TAMARA BYKOVA (USSR)

Event: Women's high jump
Olympic record: 1.97m Sara Simeoni (Italy) 1980

Fact file:
Born 21 December 1958
Ht 5 ft 10 in. Wt 139 lb
World Cup runner-up 1981, European runner-up 1982
World champion 1983
Set world record of 2.04 metres in 1983

BRENDAN FOSTER: One of the most compelling sights in the LA Games will be the continuing duel between high-jump queens Tamara Bykova and West Germany's Ulrike Meyfarth, the 1972 Olympic champion who has made a spectacular return to the athletics arena. They have been having a game of musical chairs with the world high-jump record. Ulrike lifted it to 2.02 metres when pipping Tamara in the 1982 European championships in Athens. They both pushed it up to 2.03 metres in London in August, 1983, shortly after the Russian girl had captured the world title in Helsinki, with Ulrike in second place. Then, just four days later, Tamara soared 26 cm above her own height to become outright world record holder at 2.04 m. Half Russian and half Greek, Tamara is 10 cm (4 inches) shorter than the gangling West German and believes that a 2.10 metres high jump is possible in the near future. Both are magnificent competitors, but never allow their rivalry to interfere with a warm friendship that has developed during their hours of battling against each other. I am certain both girls will capture a lot of hearts before the LA Games are over.

BERT CAMERON (Jamaica)

Event: Men's 400 metres
Olympic record: 43.86 sec Lee Evans (USA) 1968

Fact file:
Born November 16 1959
Ht 6 ft 1 in. Wt 175 lb
Commonwealth champion 1982, World champion 1983
Personal best: 44.58s

BRENDAN FOSTER: Bert Cameron has taken over the baton of the great Jamaican one-lap specialists, carrying on the tradition set by such 'golden oldies' as George Rhoden, Arthur Wint and Herb McKenley. He makes no secret of his ambition to be remembered as the greatest one-lap runner of all time. That mantle is worn at the moment by the redoubtable Lee Evans, whose astonishing world and Olympic record of 43.86 sec set in Mexico's high altitude back in 1968 has survived all attempts to wipe it from the record books. Cameron, who runs in the footsteps of Lee Evans at the University of Texas (El Paso), has shaken off a series of thigh muscle injuries to establish himself as the world's number one 400 metre runner. He has that nice, relaxed laid-back sort of personality that typifies West Indians, but behind the easy smile there is a steely determination. Bert loves running, and loves winning. West German Erwin Skamrahl could be a threat to Cameron if he can reproduce his peak form of 1983, when he crashed through the 45.00 sec barrier for the first time with an impressive clocking of 44.50 sec.

Opposite
Tamara Bykova: she's for the high jump

ERNESTO CANTO (Mexico)

Event: Men's 20 km walk
Olympic record: 1 hr 23 min 35.5 sec Maurizio Damilano (ITA) 1980

Fact file:
Born October 18 1959
Ht 5 ft 7 in. Wt 128 lb
1983 Pan American champion, 1983 World champion
Personal best: 1 hr 19 min 0.2 sec.

BRENDAN FOSTER: Walkers are a dedicated breed but they don't come more determined and committed than Ernesto Canto. He trains for eight hours every day of his life in his lonely quest for glory. He is a physical education teacher back home in Mexico but was given three years leave of absence in 1981 so that he could set his sights on the world and Olympic titles. He pulled off the first leg of his ambitious double in the world championships in Helsinki, setting off at blistering speed and teasing his rivals with sudden changes of pace until only muscular Czech Jozef Pribilinec could stay with him. They had a titanic duel over the last third of the course, with Canto surviving a warning for 'lifting' before going away to win by just ten seconds. Pribilinec avenged this defeat in the prestigious Lugano Cup competition in September, 1983, and the stage is set for a deciding battle in Los Angeles when defending champion Maurizio Damilano's Olympic record seems sure to be beaten out of sight by half a dozen walkers capable of cracking the 1 hour 20 minute barrier. Poland's Zdzislaw Klapa will be a strong medal contender if he can maintain the form he showed at the back-end of the 1983 season when he lowered his personal best to 1 hr 19 min 55.07 sec.

SEBASTIAN COE (Great Britain)

Event: Men's 800 metres
Olympic record: 1m 43.50s Alberto Juantorena (CUB) 1976

Fact file:
Born September 29 1956
Ht 5 ft 9 in. Wt 122 lb
Olympic 1500 metres champion 1980
Olympic 800 metres runner-up 1980
Set world 800 metres record of 1 min 41.73 sec in 1981

BRENDAN FOSTER: It will be a tragedy if Seb is unable to reach peak fitness for the challenge of the LA Olympics following the glandular problems that made 1983 such a year of misery for him. Knowing Seb as I do, I believe he will go to Los Angeles only if he feels he can do himself and the Great Britain team justice. He is one of the most gifted athletes ever to set foot on a running track, and has the ability to conquer all-comers if he is anywhere near his best form. His appearance on the starting-line will strike fear into the hearts of the finest runners and I am jumping in with the prediction that he will win the 800 metres gold medal to go with the silver he collected in Moscow in 1980. The stopwatch has proved he is the fastest two-lap specialist of all time but his performances in the major championships have brought criticism of his tactical judgment. The Olympic Memorial Stadium in Los Angeles is the ideal stage on which to re-establish himself as one of the masters of the track.

Following pages
Ernesto Canto: thumbs up for the walking master

Sebastian Coe: good enough to beat all-comers

Opposite
Bert Cameron: has the gold medal in his lap

EAMONN COGHLAN (Eire)

Event: Men's 5000 metres
Olympic record: 13 min 20.34 sec Brendan Foster (GB) 1976

Fact file:
Born November 21 1952
Ht 5ft 9¾in. Wt 139 lb
European 1500 metres runner-up 1978
World Cup 5000 metres winner 1981, World champion 1983
Personal best 13 min 19.13 sec

BRENDAN FOSTER: One thing's for sure — the Olympic 5000 metres record I set in a heat of the 1976 Games in Montreal will not survive. The ease of his victory in the world championship final in Helsinki proved conclusively that Eamonn Coghlan has adjusted to his switch to the longer distance after establishing himself as one of the world's top milers. He has such an electrifying finish that if he is in contention with 300 metres to go, I would back him to take the gold medal. It would be a marvellous moment for Eamonn if he could pull it off because for years he has given the impression of being able to win major races only on the American indoor circuit, where he has well earned the nickname Chairman of the Boards. His triumph in Helsinki will have given him all the confidence in the world. If dreams come true, then Britain would be picking up gold medals in the 800, 1500 and 5000 metres. David Moorcroft will be untouchable in the 5000 if he can reproduce the form he showed in 1982 when setting the magnificent world record of 13 min 00.41 sec. I fear, however, that his enforced lay-off during 1983 will have robbed him of some of his speed and sharpness, although I'll be keeping my fingers crossed that he proves me wrong. Thomas Wessinhage, the doctor on the go from West Germany, will loom as a last-lap threat to them all if he can keep pace with the leaders, as Moorcroft, American Doug Padilla, Russian Dmitriy Dmitriev, East German Werner Schildhauer, Finn Martti Vainio, Portugal's wildly unpredictable Fernando Mamede and a rush of Africans try to drain the finishing power out of 'kicker' Coghlan. Both Coghlan and Moorcroft had a winter of discontent coming into Olympic year. Eamonn suffered a stress fracture, and David was still being dogged by the after-effects of hepatitis. It all adds to the uncertainty of what should be a classic 5000 metres final in Los Angeles.

ALBERTO COVA (ITALY)

Event: Men's 10,000 metres
Olympic record: 27 min 38.4 sec Lasse Viren (FIN) 1972

Fact file:
Born December 1 1958
Ht 5 ft 10 in. Wt 128 lb
European champion 1982, world champion 1983
Personal best: 27 min 37.59 sec

BRENDAN FOSTER: Alberto Cova has a big-occasion temperament that will thrive in the electric atmosphere certain to be generated in the Olympic Stadium at Los Angeles. There are a dozen top-flight 10,000 metre specialists all about the same standard in what is a wide-open event but Cova has the edge over all of them because of his spectacular finishing kick. He produced an extraordinary burst in the 1983 world championship final in Helsinki, overtaking a cluster of rivals as he completed the last lap in 53.9 sec. Alberto is coached by Giorgio Rondelli at the Pro Patria Pierrel club (which is financed by a Milan millionaire), and he builds reserves of stamina with hard winter running across country. East Germans Werner Schildhauer and Hansjorg Kunze and Portuguese Carlos Lopes and Fernando Mamede will be trying to run the finish out of Cova, and Africa will be strongly represented by Gidamis Shahanga, Mohamed Kedir, Bekele Debele and Mike Mosyoki. We may well have a repeat climax of the world championship 10,000 metres final when you could have thrown a blanket over the first four men to finish.

Opposite
Eamonn Coghlan: an electrifying finish

Alberto Cova: has the big-occasion temperament

STEVE CRAM (Great Britain)

Event: Men's 1500 metres
Olympic record: 3 min 34.9 sec Kip Keino (KEN) 1968

Fact file:
Born October 14 1960
Ht 6 ft 1 in. Wt 152 lb
European champion 1982, Commonwealth champion 1982
World champion 1983
Personal best: 3 min 31.66 sec

BRENDAN FOSTER: Two years ago I would have been torn between selecting Seb Coe or Steve Ovett as the likely gold medallist. Both are magnificent athletes and anything they achieve in Los Angeles will not really surprise me. But they have now been overtaken as the metric mile favourite by Steve Cram, the Jarrow lad I've had the pleasure of watching grow up and develop as a world-class athlete. He has matured both mentally and physically and has the strength, speed, tactical acumen and temperament to dictate the final. Cram is the man they will all be worried about. Ovett and/or Coe could, of course, surprise us all, and there will also be strong challenges coming from Steve Scott and Sydney Maree, Said Aouita, Jose-Luiz Gonzalez and the old fox John Walker. But I think they will be racing for the silver medal behind the long-striding Cram. Here's one onlooker who will be struggling to contain his Geordie bias!

HEIKE DAUTE (East Germany)

Event: Women's long jump
Olympic record: 7.06 metres Tatjana Kolpakova (USSR) 1980

Fact file:
Born December 16 1964
Ht 5ft 10¾ in. Wt 143 lb
European junior champion 1981
World champion 1983
Personal best: 7.14 metres (7.27m wind-assisted)

BRENDAN FOSTER: I was impressed by Heike Daute's attitude as well as her ability during the world championships in Helsinki. No sooner had she caused a stunning upset by winning the world title than she was talking about setting an Olympic gold medal as her next target. It was almost chilling to see such confidence in an eighteen-year-old and she can only get better. Her personal best leap of 7.14 metres was achieved when jumping into a three-metres-a-second headwind. Anisoara Cusmir — Romanian holder of the world record, with a phenomenal leap of 7.43 metres — is the obvious danger to Heike, and Carol Lewis, Carl's sister, will be going all out to improve on her third place in the world championships. Britain's Bev Kinch could cause a few surprises if she can continue to show the improvement that lifted her into the top bracket in 1983.

Following pages
Steve Cram: the metric mile favourite

Heike Daute: a teenager going a long way

ROB DE CASTELLA (Australia)

Event: Men's marathon
Olympic record: 2 hr 09 min 55.0 sec Waldemar Cierpinski (GDR) 1976

Fact file:
Born February 27 1957
Ht 5ft 10¾ in. Wt 143 lb
Commonwealth champion 1982
World champion 1983
Personal best: 2 hr 08 min 19.0 sec

BRENDAN FOSTER: Rob de Castella is a warm, likeable character but ice runs through his veins when he is competing and I expect to see him take command in the last third of what promises to be one of the greatest marathon races ever staged. He has proved himself able to handle any pace and any situation. Tanzanians Juma Ikangaa and Gidamis Shahanga tried to break him with a blistering pace in the Commonwealth Games and failed. The Japanese queued up to take turns to try to run the finish out of him in the 1981 Fukuoka classic and failed. Carlos Lopes shadowed him in the 1983 Rotterdam marathon with the idea of outsprinting him in the final stages — and failed. 'Deek' never looked anything but a winner in the world championships in Helsinki, and has since been pouring all his considerable concentration and intelligence into preparing for the race of a lifetime in Los Angeles. Ranged against him will be the greatest field of marathon runners ever assembled, including the world's fastest marathon man, Alberto Salazar, who is hoping to be back to full fitness after the bronchial problems that curtailed his running programme in 1983. East German Waldemar Cierpinski, the man to whom the Olympics is the supreme challenge, will be bidding for a historic hat-trick of victories, European champion Gerard Nijboer will carry the Dutch banner and Japanese hopes rest at the feet of Toshihiko Seko and Takeshi Soh. The Africans, including latest Kenyan sensation Joseph Nzau, are certain to have a big say in the pacemaking, and Britain's Hugh Jones will be hoping to go one better than silver medallists Sam Ferris (1932), Ernie Harper (1936), Tom Richards (1948) and Basil Heatley (1964). Rod Dixon, my old track rival from New Zealand, has stepped up to marathon running in impressive style and will renew his rivalry with Geoff Smith, the American-based Briton he pipped by just nine seconds in the dramatic 1983 New York marathon. But about two hours, eight minutes after the starting gun has fired I expect to see Rob de Castella confirming that he is the undisputed king of the road.

MARY DECKER (United States)

Events: Women's 1500 and 3000 metres
Olympic 1500m record: 3 min 56.6 sec Tatyana Kazankina (USSR) 1980

Fact file:
Born August 4 1958
Ht 5 ft 6 in. Wt 107 lb
Pan American 1500m champion 1979
World 1500 and 3000m champion 1983
Personal bests: 3 min 57.12 sec (1500m); 8 min 34.62 sec (3000m)

BRENDAN FOSTER: Marvellous Mary Decker is the greatest advertisement for women's athletics since Fanny Blankers-Koen was burning up the cinders back in the 1940s. Mary deserves a place in the *Guinness Book of Records* for the way she has overcome the sort of injury problems that would have made anybody of lesser spirit and determination seek the sanctuary of a wheelchair. It seems only yesterday that we were watching in awe as fourteen-year-old Mary, pigtails flying, was running for the United States and beating the top Russians over 800 metres. That was eleven years ago and we wondered what incredible feats she would perform when she grew up. But her career seemed cruelly ended almost before it had begun by a succession of leg injuries. She underwent a series of operations that have left her legs criss-crossed with scars but she has emerged from her long tunnel of distress as the remarkable runner she promised to become as a precocious youngster. Her 1500/3000 metres double in the 1983 world championships was a terrific confidence-booster for all Western women athletes who had got it into their heads that the Russians, East Germans and Eastern European women were unbeatable. It's going to be harder for Mary to make it a 'Double Decker' in Los Angeles where the 3000 metres will be added to the women's Olympic programme for the first time. Her magnificent performances in Helsinki have alerted the Eastern bloc athletes to her immense ability and they are certain to 'gang up' on her in a bid to run the finishing strength out of her suspect legs. But Mary is above all a born winner and she will boldly race from the front in an all-out effort to dictate both the 1500 and 3000 metre finals. Mildred 'Babe' Didrikson was the darling of the 1932 Games in Los Angeles. The scene is set for Mary Decker to take over as the LA84 Queen of the Games.

Opposite
Rob de Castella: the marathon man they all follow

Mary Decker: all set to become Queen of the Games

YEKATERINA FESENKO (USSR)

Event: Women's 400m hurdles
World record: 54.02 sec Anna Ambrozene (USSR) 1983

Fact file:
Born March 10 1956
Ht 5 ft 6 in. Wt 125 lb
World champion 1983
Personal best: 54.14 sec

BRENDAN FOSTER: The women's 400 metres hurdles makes its debut on the Olympic programme in Los Angeles. It's a difficult event to analyse because new talent is being drawn to it all the time. I'm playing safe by predicting victory for Yekaterina Fesenko, who won the world championship final in Helsinki in impressive style and talked afterwards of getting her time down to 53 seconds. She has made rapid progress since finishing seventh in the 1982 European championships — won by Sweden's Ann-Louise Skoglund who could achieve only sixth in Helsinki. The Russians have tremendous strength in depth in the event, and world record holder Anna Ambrozene is certain to make a strong challenge for the gold medal after being overtaken on the line by Fesenko in the world championship final. East Germany's Ellen Fielder looked a likely winner of the world title until fading on the run-in after the final hurdle. She will be a threat to the Russians if she can improve her finishing drive.

GREG FOSTER (United States)

Event: Men's 110 metres hurdles
Olympic record: 13.24 sec Rod Milburn (USA) 1972

Fact file:
Born August 4 1958
Ht 6 ft 3 in. Wt 195 lb
World Cup winner 1981, World champion 1983
Personal best: 13.03 sec

BRENDAN FOSTER: Greg Foster is a fine successor to Renaldo Nehemiah, the man who brought new horizons to hurdling before switching to professional football. Foster has excellent hurdling technique and is a top-flight sprinter, with a personal best 100 metres time of 10.28 sec. For several seasons he ran in the shadow of the great Nehemiah but is now a track superstar in his own right and firmly established himself as the world's No 1 high hurdler in Helsinki. He also has courage to go with his talent as he proved in the world championship final when he kept his discipline and determination after clattering the last three hurdles. His momentum was sufficient to hold off the stirring challenge from Finland's much-improved Arto Bryggare. Sam Turner and Tony Campbell are among a cluster of world-ranked American hurdlers who will be trying to make it a 1-2-3 clean sweep for Uncle Sam but Bryggare, defending Olympic champion Thomas Munkelt and Canada's Commonwealth champion Mark McKoy will be striving to break the US monopoly. Foster is certain to threaten the 13-second barrier in his bid to clinch the gold.

Following pages
Yekaterina Fesenko: hurdling for gold

Greg Foster: out of the shadows

Marlies Gohr: head-to-head duel with Evelyn Ashford

MARLIES GOHR (East Germany)

Event: Women's 100 metres
Olympic record: 11.01 sec Annegret Richter (West Germany) 1976

Fact file:
Born March 21 1958
Ht 5ft 5in. Wt 119 lb
World Cup winner 1977, European champion 1978
Olympic silver medallist 1980, European champion 1982
World champion 1983
Personal best: 10.81 sec

BRENDAN FOSTER: The head-to-head clash between Marlies Gohr and Evelyn Ashford promises to be one of the highlights of the Olympics, provided the American has fully recovered from the hamstring injury that forced her to pull up painfully in the world championship final. There is hardly anything to choose between them when they are both at their peak. Evelyn beat Marlies in the 1979 and 1981 World Cups and captured the world record with a 10.79 sec clocking at altitude. Marlies left Evelyn trailing in the US-East Germany match in Los Angeles in June, 1983, and her 10.81 sec dash is the fastest time ever recorded by a woman at sea-level. They have contrasting styles. Evelyn has been described as a 'running tadpole' because of the way she splays her feet when going flat out. She almost glides along the track, while the upright, quick-striding Marlies powers towards the tape. The end product from both of them is remarkable speed, and whoever strikes gold in the 100 metres in LA will justifiably be able to call herself the fastest woman on earth.

ZDZISLAW HOFFMAN (Poland)

Event: Men's triple jump
Olympic record: 17.39m Viktor Saneyev (USSR) 1968

Fact file:
Born August 27 1959
Ht 6ft 2¾in. Wt 174 lb
World champion 1983
Personal best: 17.42 metres

BRENDAN FOSTER: The triple jump has suddenly become an event that has captured public interest and imagination. Its popularity is due in no small measure to the fun and warmth that bouncing Willie Banks has brought to the pre-jump preparation, when he virtually demands — and gets — audience participation from the hand-clapping spectators. There are some critics (and competitors) who feel that Willie's amiable antics cause an irritating distraction but there can be no doubt that he has turned the triple jump from a virtually ignored event into one of the most compelling on the track and field programme. Willie is certain to be pulling out all the stops in a bid to win in front of his home crowd in Los Angeles but I think we may have seen his greatest efforts a couple of years back, while I sense the best is yet to come from young world champion Zdzislaw Hoffman. He is well equipped to carry on the fine Polish tradition in the triple jump established by two-times Olympic champion Jozef Szmidt. I am convinced that the Olympic record set by the legendary Viktor Saneyev at altitude in Mexico in 1968 is bound to go in what is certain to be a marvellous competition. European and Commonwealth champion Keith Connor could easily destroy the confidence of his rivals if he can reproduce the world-beating form that suddenly deserted him during 1983. Australian Ken Lorraway is the 'kangaroo man' of the event, who at his best is a medal prospect, and there are a dozen top-class Russians battling for a place in the LA team as they try to follow in the footsteps of the Master, Saneyev. Looming as a threat to all of them is the unpredictable but talented Nigerian Ajayi Agbebaku. One moment of inspiration from any one of them could settle the gold medal and catch everybody else on the hop!

PATRIZ ILG (West Germany)

Event: 3000 metres steeplechase
Olympic record: 8 min 08.0 sec Anders Garderud (SWE) 1976

Fact file:
Born December 5 1957
Ht 5 ft 8 in. Wt 139 lb
European champion 1982, World champion 1983
Personal best: 8 min 15.06 sec

BRENDAN FOSTER: The 'kick' finishers will be out in force in the 3000 metres steeplechase and any stragglers could get trampled on in the rush when the bell rings to signal the last lap. This promises to be one of the most spectacular races of the Games, with perhaps five or six runners in striking distance of gold approaching the water jump for the last time. I've selected Patriz Ilg as the likely winner because of his scorching finishing speed that took him to victory in the European and World championship finals. However, he had better be prepared for tougher opposition this time from America's 'head waiter' Henry Marsh, who fell at the final hurdle when delivering his usual late challenge in the world championships. Finland's Tommy Ekblom, Kenyan Kip Rono and Britain's unpredictable Colin Reitz can be expected to set a pulsating pace in a bid to break the favourites, but in the final rush for gold Ilg and Marsh should show just ahead of a fast-finishing cluster of rivals including Pole Boguslaw Maminski, Frenchman Joseph Mahmoud and Italian Mariano Scartezzini. My mouth waters at the prospect of what is going to be a classic race.

BETTINE JAHN (East Germany)

Event: Women's 100 metres hurdles
Olympic record: 12.56 sec Vera Komisova (USSR) 1980

Fact file:
Born August 3 1958
Ht 5 ft 7 in. Wt 132 lb
World champion 1983
Personal best: 12.42 sec (12.35s wind-assisted)

BRENDAN FOSTER: Bettine Jahn has made tremendous improvement since finishing seventh in the 1980 Moscow Olympics 100 metres hurdles final when running under her maiden name of Gartz. Her superiority in the world championships final in Helsinki was so clear-cut that she will go to Los Angeles as a very warm favourite. A following wind robbed her of a world record in Helsinki. She has good basic sprinter's speed and a hurdling technique that has been sharpened by expert coaching. Bettine's strongest opposition seems likely to come from her East German team-mate Kerstin Knabe and Poland's Lucyna Kalek could cause an upset if she can recover the form that took her to the European title in 1982. Britain's hopes will be carried by Shirley Strong, fifth in the world championship final and getting better with every outing. The legendary Mildred 'Babe' Didrikson won the high hurdles for the United States in LA in 1932 (then an 80 metres course), but it's unlikely that their number one hurdler — Pan American champion Benita Fitzgerald — can win for the host country this time against the all-conquering Eastern Europeans.

Patriz Ilg: a 'kicker' in the steeplechase

Bettine Jahn (nearest camera): vastly improved

Marita Koch: can add to her glittering collection

MARITA KOCH
(East Germany)

Event: Women's 200 metres
Olympic record: 22.03 sec Barbel Wockel (GDR) 1980

Fact file:
Born February 18 1957
Ht 5ft 7¼in. Wt 139 lb
European 400m champion 1978 and 1982
World Cup winner 400m, 2nd 200m 1979
Olympic 400m champion 1980 in a record 48.88 sec
World 200m champion and 100m runner-up 1983
Set world 200m record of 21.71 sec in 1979

BRENDAN FOSTER: One of the greatest all-round sprinters in the history of women's athletics, Marita Koch has the speed and the talent to challenge for gold in whichever events she decides to participate. I feel her best chance of adding to her glittering collection of major titles lies in the 200 metres now that Jarmila Kratochvilova has emerged as such a power in what was her No 1 event, the 400 metres. Like her team-mate Marlies Gohr in the 100 metres, Marita will be fearing American rocketgirl Evelyn Ashford if she is at peak fitness. Evelyn has been just about unbeatable over the distance for the past five years and the last time she and Marita met at 200 metres in the 1979 World Cup the Californian girl emerged as a convincing winner. However, the memory of her breakdown in the 1983 world championships will haunt Evelyn, and will give Marita a psychological advantage. Reigning Olympic champion Barbel Wockel, the winner in Montreal and Moscow, has been showing signs of recapturing her old speed and sparkle and just might make a bid for an astonishing hat-trick. Merlene Ottey, the Commonwealth champion from Jamaica, will also be a strong contender for a medal and Britain's Kathy Cook has a big-occasion temperament that could lift her to a challenging performance.

JARMILA KRATOCHVILOVA
(Czechoslovakia)

Events: Women's 400 and 800 metres
Olympic records:
400 metres — 48.88 sec Marita Koch (GDR) 1980
800 metres — 1 min 53.5 sec Nadezhda Olizarenko (USSR) 1980

Fact file:
Born January 26 1951
Ht 5 ft 7 in. Wt 136 lb
Olympic silver medallist 400 metres 1980
World Cup 400 metres winner 1981, 2nd 200 metres
European 400 metres silver medallist 1982
World champion 400 and 800 metres 1983
World record holder at 400m (47.99 sec) and 800m (1 min 53.28 sec)

BRENDAN FOSTER: The phenomenal Jarmila Kratochvilova proved in the 1983 world championships that she could do 'the impossible' by winning the 400 and 800 metres, even though the two events virtually overlapped. She finished a comfortable first in her 400 metres semi-final in 51.08 sec and then just thirty-three minutes later lined up for the final of the 800 metres, which she won in convincing style. The next day she completed the double by winning the 400 metres in a mind-blowing world record of 47.99 sec. Jarmila is a heavily muscled lady, which makes her the target for a lot of cynical remarks, but the fact cannot be avoided that she is an extraordinary competitor who has brought new dimensions to women's athletics. On paper there seems no way she can repeat her world championship double in Los Angeles because the two finals are scheduled for the same afternoon. But 'Queen Kratch' has already made it clear that the word 'impossible' does not exist as far as she is concerned. It would be an incredible performance by a woman who did not do better than 55 seconds for 400 metres until she was twenty-five. Her long-standing coach Miroslav Kvac will study the Olympic schedule before deciding her programme, and it just might be that she will aim for a 200/400 double. There was even talk of this amazing athlete stepping up to challenge Mary Decker in the 1500 metres. Whatever her final targets, it will take exceptional performances from rivals like Marita Koch and her team-mate Tatjana Kocembova to prevent her bowing out of athletics with two Olympic gold medals — and possibly a third in the 4 x 400 metres relay in which the rivalry between the East Germans and the Czechs will guarantee this being a classic race.

CARL LEWIS (United States)

Events: Men's 100, 200 metres and long jump
Olympic records:
100m — 9.95 sec Jim Hines (USA) 1968
200m — 19.83 sec Tommie Smith (USA) 1968
Long-jump — 8.90m Bob Beamon (USA) 1968

Fact file:
Born July 1 1961
Ht 6 ft 2 in. Wt 180 lb
World Cup long-jump winner 1981
World champion 100m and long jump 1983
Personal bests:
100 metres — 9.97 sec (world non-altitude best)
200 metres — 19.75 sec (world non-altitude best)
Long jump — 8.79 metres (world non-altitude best)

BRENDAN FOSTER: Frederick Carlton Lewis has made such a spectacular impact on world athletics in the last two years that you get the feeling he has only to turn up at the Olympic Stadium in Los Angeles to repeat the stupendous Jesse Owens feat of winning four gold medals. Of course, it isn't going to be anything like as easy as that, but it will be more of a surprise if he doesn't reach his four-gold target than if he does. I can see no danger to him in the long-jump, where he clearly has the ability to become the first man to beat the 30 foot barrier and so remove Bob Beamon's stunning record from the world and Olympic books. Calvin Smith, world champion at 200 metres, is the man who stands between Lewis and a sprint double. But Lewis has the target of four Olympic titles fixed firmly in his mind and will have the accelerator pushed right down to the floor in his bid for golden glory. When he is at peak power the new superman of the track is out on his own and will not allow Smith to catch him napping on the bend, as happened during an end-of-season race in Europe last year. His 'easiest' gold medal will come in the sprint relay when, provided there are no hitches with the baton-passing, the United States quartet — with the awesome Lewis running the anchor leg — could improve on the 37.86 sec world record they set in the 1983 world championships in Helsinki.

TIINA LILLAK (Finland)

Event: Women's javelin
Olympic record: 68.40 metres Maria Colon (CUB) 1980

Fact file:
Born April 15 1961
Ht 5ft 10¾in. Wt 160 lb
World champion 1983
Set world record of 74.76 metres in 1983

BRENDAN FOSTER: Tiina Lillak showed a true champion's competitive qualities when she produced a title-winning effort off her last throw in the 1983 world championships in front of her home crowd in Helsinki. Britain's Fatima Whitbread had led throughout the competition with a magnificent first throw that finally brought her a silver medal and marked her as an Olympic threat. Fatima, hoping to overcome a recurring back problem, and Tessa Sanderson will be aiming to win Britain's first Olympic medal(s) in the throwing events since hammerman Malcolm Nokes collected a silver back in 1924. But Tiina will be the one to beat and there will also be tough opposition from Greek pair Sofia Sakorafa and Anna Verouli, the European champion who has reportedly been hitting the 75-metre mark in training. East Germany will be powerfully represented by Antje Kempe and Petra Felke and Cuba's Maria Colon will be doing her best to retain the title she won with her first throw in the 1980 Moscow final.

Opposite
Jarmila Kratochvilova: a phenomenal competitor

Tiina Lillak: a thrower in the best Finnish traditions

Opposite
Carl Lewis: out to emulate Jesse Owens

SERGEY LITVINOV (USSR)

Event: Men's hammer
Olympic record: 81.80m Yuri Sedykh (USSR) 1980

Fact file:
Born January 23 1958
Ht 5ft 10¾in. Wt 213 lb
World Cup winner 1979
Olympic silver medallist 1980, World champion 1983
Set world record of 84.14 metres in 1983

BRENDAN FOSTER: Sergey Litvinov eclipsed The Master, Yuri Sedykh, in the 1983 world championships after taking his compatriot's world record earlier in the year. It ended an astonishing record of supremacy by Sedykh, the Olympic champion in 1976 and 1980 and European gold medallist in 1978 and 1982. The Russian strongarm men can be expected to dominate the hammer event in Los Angeles, with Litvinov looking well able to prevent an Olympic hat-trick by the mighty Sedykh. The hammer has become a speciality event for the Russians, who have a dozen potential medallists in the world rankings. They have captured the Olympic title five times in the last six Olympics, and Litvinov can maintain the winning standards. Anatoliy Bondarchuk, the 1972 Olympic champion and Sedykh's mentor and coach, calls the stylish, lightning-fast Litvinov 'the most complete thrower of all time.' An Army officer with an insatiable appetite for reading Russian classics, Litvinov has been preparing for the Olympics in the seclusion of a Black Sea training camp, where it is rumoured that he has been continually peppering the 85-metre mark. Igor Nikulin (son of Yuri, who was fourth in the 1964 Olympics) has been concentrating on the hammer throw since he was just thirteen years old and is making the sort of progress that marks him as a future champion. But he has still got some way to go to catch the 'Big Two,' Litvinov and Sedykh. World championship bronze medallist Zdzislaw Kwasny, of Poland, is the biggest threat to a Russian clean sweep.

ED MOSES (United States)

Event: Men's 400 metres hurdles
Olympic record: 47.64 sec Ed Moses (USA) 1976

Fact file:
Born August 31 1955
Ht 6 ft 2 in. Wt 170 lb
Olympic champion 1976
World Cup winner 1977/79/81
World champion 1983
Set new world record at 47.02 sec in 1983

BRENDAN FOSTER: Who will finish second? That seems the only subject for debate in the 400 metres hurdles in which 'The King,' Ed Moses, should show why he is rated one of the most accomplished athletes of the century. It will be no surprise if Moses underlines his presence at the Games by becoming the first man to break the 47-seconds barrier. He has created a quite incredible record of invincibility, winning more than ninety races in succession since his last defeat by West German Harald Schmid back in 1977. Moses has avenged that defeat many times over, and would have been a certainty to retain his Olympic title in Moscow in 1980 but for the boycott that robbed him of the chance to emulate Glenn Davis's unique record of two successive gold medals in the 'man-killer' event. All of us in athletics will applaud a Moses victory: he stands for everything that is good and right about the sport. He is an outspoken critic of drug abuse, and gives the perfect example to young athletes with his dedicated approach and his sporting attitude. Who will come second? I plump for Harald Schmid, who manages to shine as a brilliant athlete despite having to live continually in the shadow of the one and only Moses.

Opposite
Sergey Litvinov: strongarm man of the hammer event

Ed Moses: an incredible record of invincibility

RAMONA NEUBERT (East Germany)

Event: Women's heptathlon
Replaces the pentathlon in the Olympic programme

Fact file:
Born July 26 1958
Ht 5 ft 8 in. Wt 141 lb
European champion 1982
World champion 1983
Set world record of 6836 points in 1983

BRENDAN FOSTER: Ramona Neubert has made the seven-event heptathlon her own property since it replaced the five-event pentathlon in 1982 as the major test for women's all-round athletes. The events are, first day: 100 metres hurdles, high jump, shot and 200 metres; second day: long jump, javelin and 800 metres. Ramona, needless to say, has exceptional all-round talent, and there are no weaknesses in her repertoire. She is a world-class sprinter and has developed strength in the field events since the 1980 Olympics, when she finished fourth in the pentathlon. East Germany made a clean sweep of the medals in the 1983 world championships, and will be looking to repeat their monopoly in Los Angeles. Britain's Judy Livermore could give them a tough time if she can maintain the improvement she showed in 1983, and Australian Glynis Nunn will be a medal contender if she can recapture the form she flourished when winning the 1982 Commonwealth championship.

MARTINA OPITZ (East Germany)

Event: Women's discus
Olympic record: 69.96 metres Evelin Jahl (GDR) 1980

Fact file:
Born December 12 1960
Ht 5 ft 10 in. Wt 176 lb
World champion 1983
Personal best: 70.26 metres, 1983

BRENDAN FOSTER: Martina Opitz had no previous major event experience before competing in the 1983 world championships in Helsinki where she was so dominant in the discus circle that she was immediately installed as favourite for the Olympic crown. Three of her throws in Helsinki were beyond the best of any of her competitors in a strong field that included Russian world record holder Galina Savinkova, who has not been able to repeat her astonishing 73.26 metre form outside the Soviet Union. Martina is also a top-class shot-putter. She has the strength and style to monopolize the discus event for several years, particularly if she can maintain the sort of improvement she showed in 1983 when she increased her personal best by six metres. Bulgarians Maria Petkova and European champion Tzvetanka Khristova are both potential medallists when at their peak and Russia will be looking to Galina Murashova to improve on her silver medal performance in the world championships. Galina Savinkova will be watched with interest to see if she can produce anything like her world record form after a disappointing display in Helsinki when she failed to get over 60 metres in the final. Gisela Beyer, younger sister of men's shot-put favourite Udo, will be hoping to complete a family double.

Martina Opitz: can dominate in the discus

Opposite
Ramona Neubert: exceptional all-round strength

Tom Petranoff: likes the sun on his back

TOM PETRANOFF (United States)

Event: Men's javelin
Olympic record: 94.58m Miklos Nemeth (HUN) 1976

Fact file:
Born April 8 1958
Ht 6 ft 2 in. Wt 204 lb
World championship runner-up 1983
Set world record of 99.72 metres in 1983

BRENDAN FOSTER: Tom Petranoff and world champion Detlef Michel continue their long-throwing javelin duel in the Olympics with the 100-metre barrier looming as a possible target. Petranoff beat the left-handed East German in Los Angeles in the early summer of 1983 but Michel got his revenge in the world championships in Helsinki. Rain was pelting down during the world championships, providing conditions that Petranoff hates, and to add to his misery he was barred from using his favourite Held Custom Series 111 javelin because it was not approved by the authorities. He should have the sun on his back in LA, when he will be bidding to become only the second American to win the javelin gold medal (Cyrus Young was champion in 1952). Petranoff is at home in California where he set his sensational world record of 99.72 metres in May 1983. Defending Olympic champion Dainis Kula and his Russian team-mate Heino Puuste will be providing tough opposition and the whole of Finland will be hoping and praying for a winning throw from Pentti Sinersaari in the stadium where the idolized Matti Jarvinen captured one of Finland's five javelin gold medals in 1932.

ILONA SLUPIANEK (East Germany)

Event: Women's shot
Olympic record: 22.41m Ilona Slupianek (GDR) 1980

Fact file:
Born September 24 1956
Ht 5ft 10¾in. Wt 206 lb
European champion 1978/1982
World Cup winner 1977/1979/1981
Olympic champion 1980
World championship bronze medallist 1983
Set a world record of 22.45 metres in 1980

BRENDAN FOSTER: Provided that she is fully recovered from the tendon injury that handicapped her in the 1983 world championships, there seems little doubt that Ilona Slupianek will retain the Olympic title she won in Moscow by the biggest margin on record. She was a champion in disgrace in 1977, when a doping test after she had won the European Cup Final proved she had been taking anabolic steroids. A ban on her was lifted after less than a year and she returned to the international arena, where she has consistently shown herself to be in a class of her own. Her closest rival throughout her career has been 34-year-old Czechoslovakian Helena Fibingerova. She took full advantage of Slupianek's power cut in Helsinki to at last win a major title after a succession of silver medals in the shadow of the East German. Also in contention for the championship if Slupianek and Fibingerova are at less than their best will be East German Helma Knorscheidt, Russians Nunu Abashidze and Natalia Lisovskaya and Romanian Mihaela Loghin.

DALEY THOMPSON (Great Britain)

Event: Men's decathlon
Olympic record: 8618 points Bruce Jenner (USA) 1976

Fact file:
Born July 30 1958
Ht 6ft 0½in. Wt 195 lb
Commonwealth champion 1978/1982
Olympic champion 1980
European champion 1982
World champion 1983
Personal best: 8743 points in 1982

BRENDAN FOSTER: Daley Thompson has a mental picture drawn that shows him becoming the first decathlete in history collecting a third successive gold medal at the 1988 Olympics in Seoul. And when Daley makes up his mind to do something, it will need a spectacular effort to stop him! He is one of the greatest competitors in the history of his sport and he breaks the hearts and spirits of his rivals with a mixture of his athletic talent and an iron will. The ten events in the decathlon are, first day: 100 metres, long jump, shot, high jump, 400 metres; second day: 110 metres hurdles, discus, pole vault, javelin and 1500 metres. The final event reveals the only weakness in Daley's armour but by the time he's reluctantly pulling his heavy frame round the track on that tortuous 1500 metres run I am sure that as usual he will have virtually got his second gold medal in the bag, on the way to his ambitious hat-trick. West Germans Jurgen Hingsen and Siggy Wentz are as gifted as Thompson but lack his driving determination when the pressure is at its peak. I'm convinced that Daley will be crowned the all-round king of the LA Games.

GRETE WAITZ (Norway)

Event: Women's marathon
World best: 2 hr 22 min 43 sec Joan Benoit (USA) 1983

Fact file:
Born October 1 1953
Ht 5ft 7¾in. Wt 121 lb
World cross-country champion 1978/79/80/81/83
New York marathon winner four times
London marathon winner 1983
World champion 1983
Personal best: 2 hr 25 min 29 sec, 1983

BRENDAN FOSTER: The greatest long-distance runner in the history of women's athletics, Grete Waitz can put a golden finish to her glittering career by winning the inaugural Olympic women's marathon in Los Angeles. Grete the Great has made it clear that this will be her final race in a major championship, and she will have an army of well-wishers hoping she at last gets her name into the Olympic record book. It is there that she so richly deserves to be, after the way she has lifted women's running into new realms. I have been on training runs with Grete, and can vouch for the fact that she is a supreme athlete and, like Mary Decker, a wonderful advertisement for the sport. It will be anything but easy for her in LA, where the winner will have to run nearly ten minutes faster than when Juan Carlos Zabala won the *men's* marathon the last time the Games were staged in Los Angeles in 1932. Zabala clocked 2 hr 31 min 36 sec, while the current women's world best is the 2 hr 22 min 43 sec clocking of American Joan Benoit in 1983. Among Grete's toughest rivals will be Americans Benoit, Marianne Dickerson and Julie Brown, Russian Raisa Smekhnova, Portugal's European champion Rosa Mota, West German Charlotte Teske, Canadian Jacqueline Gareau and Britain's incredible running mum Joyce Smith. But I can't see any of them stopping Grete from becoming the first Olympic 'Queen of the Road'.

Opposite
Ilona Slupianek: in a class of her own

Grete Waitz: a wonderful advertisement for athletics

Opposite
Daley Thompson: the world's greatest all-rounder

RONALD WEIGEL (East Germany)

Event: Men's 50 kilometre walk
Olympic record: 3hr 49m 24s Hartwig Gauder (GDR) 1980

Fact file:
Born May 6 1956
Ht 6 ft 1.1/2in. Wt 156 lb
World champion 1983
Personal best: 3hr 41m 31s, 1983

BRENDAN FOSTER: I was torn between selecting Ronald Weigel and Mexican pace-setter Raul Gonzalez as favourite for this longest event in the Olympic programme. I finally settled for the East German because of the confident and competent way he dealt with the Gonzalez challenge in the 1983 world championships. Gonzalez likes to maintain a quick tempo but can be overhauled in the last third of the race if anybody is able to hang on to his heels. This was the tactic that Weigel used to such good effect in Helsinki, keeping Gonzalez in sight and then applying the pressure when it was clear that the Mexican had walked himself to the edge of exhaustion. Gonzalez proved he was not too dispirited by the defeat when, the following month, he won the hotly contested Lugano Trophy 50 km event for a third time. There has been a lot of controversy at the major championships over the interpretation by some international judges as to what constitutes 'lifting'. I have seen the almost comical sight of walkers virtually running without receiving a warning from the judges, while on the other hand there have been disqualifications of other competitors who have appeared to be following the rule of 'progression by steps so taken that unbroken contact with the ground is maintained.' I hope no disputes mar the LA events when the walkers will be getting the international spotlight that they deserve.

Opposite
Ronald Weigel: ready for the long walk

PART TWO

OLYMPIC HEROES

An A to Z guide to the great Olympic champions

HAROLD ABRAHAMS
Great Britain (1899-1978)

Competing in the 1924 Games in Paris, Harold Abrahams became the first European and the only Englishman to win a gold medal in the 100 metres — a triumph that was featured in the Oscar-winning film *Chariots of Fire*. Born into a middle-class Jewish family in Bedford, he was an exceptional all-rounder who monopolized the sprint events and the long jump during his four years at Cambridge University. His family was steeped in athletics. One brother was an international-class long-jumper, and another served the British track and field team for many years as medical officer.

Abrahams made his Olympic debut in Antwerp in 1920, when he represented Britain in four events —

Harold Abrahams (No 419): winning in Paris

the 100 and 200 metres, long jump and the sprint relay. He returned home from Antwerp empty-handed but richer for the experience, and with an ambitious plan to improve his training technique so that he could not only compete but *win* at world level. Flying Scot Eric Liddell was expected to be one of his greatest rivals in Paris but withdrew from the 100 metres on religious grounds because the final was to be staged on a Sunday. However, Abrahams still faced tough opposition, particularly from crack Americans Jackson Scholz and defending champion and world record holder Charley Paddock.

After equalling the Olympic record of 10.6 sec in both the second round and the semi-final, Abrahams quickly got into his long stride in the final and held a commanding lead at the halfway point. Scholz made a tremendous effort to overhaul him in the last third of a classic race but was still a metre behind in second place as Harold powered through the tape with the clock again stopping at 10.6 sec.

Scholz got his revenge when winning the 200 metres. Abrahams, tired and sluggish, trailed in sixth and last, but he regained his drive and determination in time to help Britain to a silver medal in the sprint relay. His distinguished career was brought to a painful and premature end the following year when he broke a leg while competing in the long jump, an event in which he held the English native record for an astonishing span of thirty-three years. He continued to serve athletics as a respected administrator, and became an authoritative writer, statistician and broadcaster who was a regular contributor to BBC radio right up until his death in 1978, at which time he was president of the AAA.

JOHN AKII-BUA
Uganda (1949)

John Akii-Bua first attracted media attention during the 1972 Munich Games, when it was learnt that he was one of forty-three children, his father having eight wives. But it was soon his great talent as an athlete that took over as the main point of interest when he won the 400 metres hurdles in a world record 47.82 sec. Trailing behind him in second and third place were race favourites Ralph Mann, of the United States, and Britain's 1968 Olympic champion David Hemery. The tall, lean and lithe Ugandan revealed that he had prepared for the Olympic challenge by wearing a specially weighted 25 lb combat jacket while hurdling in training runs over the 400 metres course.

He was prevented from defending his title in 1976 by the mass African boycott of the Montreal Games, and his crown and the world record were taken over by the incomparable Ed Moses. There were disturbing rumours that he had been imprisoned during Idi Amin's tyrannical reign, and it was to the relief of his many friends in the athletics world when he turned up as an exile in West Germany in 1979. John, an accomplished decathlete, followed a crash training programme in a bid to regain his Olympic title in the 1980 Moscow Games, but his gallant attempt ended in the semi-finals.

VASILI ALEXEEV
USSR (1942)

For nearly a decade the giant Vasili Alexeev made light of the awe-inspiring title 'The World's Strongest Man'. The 23-stone Russian mining engineer won the first of two Olympic super-heavyweight weight-lifting titles in the 1972 Munich Games at the age of thirty. He retained the title in Montreal four years later, setting a world record in the clean and jerk on the way and silencing critics who said he had been ducking duels with several of his Eastern European and American rivals. This big bear of a man had his own highly individual ideas on training and was often the despair of Russian officials who preferred their sportsmen to conform. 'Only I understand what is good and right for me,' he told newsmen after his second Olympic triumph in Montreal. 'I train when I feel I should. Sometimes it is deep in the night,

Vasili Alexeev: the world's strongest man

sometimes in the morning. Sometimes I train several times in one day. Sometimes I prefer not to train at all.'

Alexeev was unbeaten in any competition for nine years from 1970 and he won eight world championships. An injury prevented him making proper preparations for the Moscow Olympics, and he had to suffer the humiliation of being jeered and whistled off the stage after failing with all three of his snatch lifts and going out of the competition without registering a single score. How are the mighty fallen!

GARY ANDERSON
United States (1939)

It has been said of Gary Anderson that he could split a hair from 100 paces with a single rifle shot. He was considered the greatest deadeye shot in the world during the 1960s, a decade during which he won eleven individual and ten team gold medals in international competition as well as Olympic titles in the free rifle event in 1964 and 1968. A rare left-hander, he was a self-taught marksman from Nebraska who reached the peak of perfection when defending his Olympic title in Mexico in 1968. The free rifle event was then rated the 'classic' of the shooting competitions and Anderson retained his crown in classic style with an Olympic and world record score of 1157 points. A total of 40 shots are fired in each of the prone, kneeling and standing positions at a target 300 metres away. The ten-point bullseye is just 10 cm in diameter and 29-year-old Anderson peppered it as if it were 10 metres wide!

IOLANDA BALAS
Romania (1936)

A tall, leggy Transylvanian, Iolanda Balas lifted women's high jumping to new heights with a long sequence of outstanding performances during a ten-year span when she completely dominated the event. She set the first of fourteen world high-jump records in July 1956 when clearing 5ft 8¾in (1.75 m) and before her injury-forced retirement in 1967 had pushed it up to 6ft 3¼in (1.91 m). She won the Olympic gold medal in 1960 and again in 1964.

Iolanda, who stood just over six foot, perfected the old-fashioned but effective 'scissors' style of jumping, and after finishing fifth in the 1956 Olympics went through an incredible run of 140 competitions without being beaten. She beat the six-foot barrier more than fifty times in an era when only five women had cleared it a handful of times between them. No other athlete has ever dominated an event for such a length of time and with such supremacy. She started high-jumping at the age of eleven and from 1953 was coached by top Romanian men's high-jumper Ion Soeter whom she married shortly after her retirement.

Iolanda Balas: set 14 world high-jump records

JOSEF BARTHEL
Luxembourg (1924)

Josef Barthel was one of the most surprised and surprising Olympic track champions of all time. He won the coveted 1500 metres gold medal in the 1952 Games in Helsinki, beating a top-class field that included world-rated runners like British master-miler Roger Bannister, American champion Bob McMillen, French-Algerian flyer Patrick El Mabrouk and German ace Werner Lueg. All of them were on paper yards faster than Barthel, and even after he had won his heat and semi-final in impressive style nobody seriously gave him a chance of winning the Blue Riband event of the Olympics — nobody, that is, with the exception of his wily coach Woldemar Gerschler, who had been the motivator of Germany's pre-war track star Rudolph Harbig and Britain's 'lone wolf' of the track, Gordon 'Puff-Puff' Pirie. Barthel followed a demanding training schedule that brought his body-weight down by thirty pounds, and Gerschler worked at sharpening his finishing speed during a thorough build-up to the Olympics. He instructed him to 'stay with the pace' and then launch an attack off the final bend.

The balding, gold-toothed little man from Luxembourg followed his race orders to perfection and was on the heels of leader Werner Lueg at the bell. He moved up to Lueg's shoulder with 200 metres to go and then unleashed a sprint that left McMillen and Lueg having to fight it out for second place. The sting had been drawn from Roger Bannister's famous 'kick' finish that was to make him the first four-minute miler two years later, and the long-striding British favourite came in a tired and disappointed fourth. Tears streamed down Barthel's face when he became the first citizen of the tiny Duchy of Luxembourg to stand on an Olympic victory rostrum. He had set a new Olympic record of 3 min 45.1 sec, more than five seconds faster than he had ever run before.

Bob Beamon: taking a walk in space

BOB BEAMON
United States (1946)

'Don't get Bob Beamon mad,' said 1960 gold medallist Ralph Boston only half jokingly as the cream of the world's long-jumpers prepared for the 1968 final in Mexico City. 'He's likely to jump clear out of the pit.' Beamon got himself mad by struggling to qualify for the final stages, scrambling through on his third and last effort after registering two no-jumps. This traumatic experience convinced Bob Beamon — at twenty-two, the youngest of the finalists — that he should pour every ounce of his energy and effort into his first jump in the final. His plan was to try to produce 'a big one' that would put his more experienced rivals under psychological pressure. He succeeded beyond his or anybody else's wildest dreams.

Beamon had clinched his place in the US team with a wind-aided leap of 27ft 6½in, the longest jump ever

recorded. It triggered a lot of conjecture as to whether in the thin, rarefied air of high-altitude Mexico he could become the first man to break the 28-foot barrier. A 6 ft 5 in high-jumper and a 9.5 sec 100 yards sprinter, the stork-legged black New Yorker was potentially the finest long-jumper in the world, but he was wildly inconsistent and unpredictable. Ranged against him in Mexico were the three well-established kings of the event: the remarkably consistent Ralph Boston; Russian Igor Ter-Ovanesyan, an Olympic veteran who was joint world record holder with Boston at 27ft 4¾in; and Welshman Lynn 'The Leap' Davies, the reigning Olympic, European and Commonwealth champion. Beamon, on a basketball and athletics scholarship at Texas-El Paso University, knew he had to pull out something mind-blowing to trump this trio of magnificent jumpers.

The sky was dark and overcast as Beamon jogged at the end of the runway getting himself mentally prepared for his first jump. It was a mind-over-matter moment because he had just seen the first three competitors register no-jumps and nerves were jangling like alarm bells. He composed himself and then set off on his 19-stride approach run, in which he generated stunning speed before hitting the take-off board with his right foot and then rising spectacularly as if launching from a trampoline. Beamon seemed to be on a space walk as his long legs scissored through a one-and-a-half-stride hitchkick. With a superhuman effort, he again propelled his slim, 6 ft 3 in, 11-stone frame forward as he landed at the far end of the sandpit and then his momentum carried him on in a series of kangaroo-like hops and bounds before he applied the brakes and came bouncing back on his spring heels to see just how much psychological damage he had managed to inflict on his rivals. It quickly became apparent that he had devastated them with just one prodigious leap.

Supported by a slight but legally acceptable following wind of two metres per second, Beamon had landed beyond the range of the electric eye of the modern measuring mechanism and the judges had to call for an old-fashioned steel tape. Beamon crouched over, watching them measure, and then suddenly started bounding back towards his team-mates with his arms raised. He stopped and kissed the ground and then looked up to the sky in a God-thanking gesture. 'Gentlemen, I believe we have just witnessed the first 28-foot long jump in history,' a veteran athletics correspondent announced to the Press box. He was right, yet wrong. The electric scoreboard revealed that Beamon had in fact cleared 8.90 metres — *29ft 2½in.*

Beamon had leapt into the twenty-first century with a jump that added an unbelievable 21 inches to the old world record. Track and field statisticians, unaware that a youngster called Carl Lewis was waiting around the corner, agreed that it was the record most likely to stand the test of time, and would still be the target for athletes in twenty-five years' time. The Olympic champion with a jump of a lifetime, Beamon abandoned plans to become a professional basketball player and toured the athletics circuit almost as a sideshow attraction. But, handicapped by hamstring problems, he was never again able to get close to his Olympic performance, and in 1973 he turned to professional athletics. 'What happened in Mexico was like a dream...a fantastic dream,' he said. Many people in athletics considered it the 'impossible dream.'

NINO BENVENUTI
Italy (1938)
The son of an Adriatic fisherman, Giovanni (Nino) Benvenuti launched a spectacularly successful career in the professional ring after winning the Olympic welterweight title in Rome in 1960. Trieste-born Benvenuti collected the Val Barker Best Stylist Trophy in the Rome Games after outpointing Britain's Jim Lloyd in the semi-finals, and Russian favourite Yuri Radonyak in the final. He was working as an insurance agent when he became Olympic champion but then switched full-time to fighting for a living and quickly came up with a winning policy. Nino was a skilful boxer with a powerful punch in either hand. He took the professional world light-middleweight title from Sandro Mazzinghi in 1965, and then two years later won the middleweight championship with a shock points victory over the vastly experienced Emile Griffith in New York.

Griffith avenged the defeat five months later but Benvenuti regained the championship in March 1968, with a unanimous 15 rounds points victory over the black American on the opening promotion at the New Madison Square Garden. The Italian idol retired in 1971 after two title-fight defeats by Argentinian Carlos Monzon. He lost just seven out of ninety professional contests.

JACK BERESFORD
Great Britain (1899)
Jack Beresford was one of the most consistent and remarkable 'Olympians' of all time. The son of a champion oarsman, he was wounded in France in the last year of the First World War but recovered to start a sculling career that has rarely if ever been equalled. He won the coveted Diamond Sculls at Henley Royal Regatta in 1920 (the first of four victories in the event), and was the hero of Henley over a span of twenty years during which he won ten major trophies. His Olympic career started in Antwerp in 1920, when he reached the final of the single sculls in which he was narrowly defeated by the great American oarsman Jack Kelly. He competed in five consecutive Olympics and was preparing for a sixth appearance in the 1940 Games when war intervened. Although weighing only a few pounds over eleven stone, Beresford built up enormous power in his arms and torso, and proof of his endurance is that he won a medal at each Olympics in which he took part, finishing with a haul of three golds and two silvers.

Born in Chiswick on New Year's Day, 1899, Beresford had his most memorable triumph in the 1936 Berlin Olympics. Partnered by his Thames Rowing Club team-mate Leslie (Dick) Southwood in the double sculls, he used his vast experience to outfox powerful German partners Joachim Pirsch and Willy Kaidel, who had beaten the British pair in one heat. The 37-year-old Beresford suggested waiting tactics for the final, and he and Southwood came from behind to beat the German favourites by two and a half lengths. He was appointed manager and coach of the Great Britain team after the Second World War, and was honoured by the IOC with the award of the Olympic Diploma of Merit.

ABEBE BIKILA
Ethiopia (1932-1973)

Abebe Bikila was a comparatively unknown force when he arrived at the start of the marathon in the 1960 Games in Rome. A little over two and a quarter hours later he was catapulted to world fame after running barefoot to an Olympic gold medal. His triumph had thrilled everybody — with the exception of the sports-shoe manufacturers! A 28-year-old private in Emperor Haile Selassie's Imperial Guard, he had been given leave to compete in Rome after winning the Ethiopian Olympic trial in 2 hr 21 min 23 sec. It was only his second run over the marathon distance and his performance at high altitude made little impression outside Ethiopia.

A vital stretch of the Rome marathon was to be staged over the cobbled stones of the historic Appian Way and when the 5 ft 10 in, 9-stone Bikila went to the starting line in bare feet few people gave him a chance of surviving the course, let alone winning the race. However, running through the moonlit streets with a smooth, economical stride, he never once looked in any kind of distress, and moved away from his well-shod rivals to become the first black African to win an Olympic title. The irony of Bikila's triumph would not have been lost on the Italian spectators as they cheered his victory in a world's best time of 2 hr 15 min 16.2 sec. He had been just three years old when his country had been invaded by Mussolini's

Abebe Bikila: the master of the marathon

troops. Now it was his turn to conquer. He became an idol in his homeland, where one of his rewards was promotion to sergeant in the Imperial Guard.

Four years later in Tokyo — this time wearing shoes — Bikila became the first marathon man ever to retain the Olympic title. He won in another new world's best time of 2 hr 12 min 11.2 sec. What made his achievement all the more remarkable is that just five weeks earlier he had been lying in a hospital operating theatre having his appendix removed. He was so fresh at the finish of the Tokyo marathon that he was able to carry out a series of exercises in the centre of the stadium, while Japan's Kokichi Tsuburaya and Britain's Basil Heatley battled for second place. Heatley managed to get in front with just 200 metres to go and poor Tsuburaya felt so humiliated at being overtaken within sight of the finishing-line that he went into a deep depression and some months later committed hara-kiri.

There was also a tragic end to the amazing Abebe Bikila story. A leg injury prevented him completing his hat-trick bid in the 1968 Olympic marathon in Mexico where victory went to his friend and countryman Mamo Wolde. A year later he was seriously injured in a car crash, and was confined to a wheelchair despite treatment at the famous Stoke Mandeville paraplegic hospital in England. He bravely took up paraplegic sport and became a master at archery, but he finally lost his battle for life when he died of a brain haemorrhage in October 1973. He was forty-one. The name of the great Abebe Bikila will always live on in Olympic legend.

FANNY BLANKERS-KOEN
Holland (1918)

As an eighteen-year-old high-jumper, Fanny Blankers-Koen finished equal sixth in the 1936 Olympics in Berlin. She was a thirty-year-old housewife and mother of two children by the time the next Games were staged in London in 1948. By then most athletes would have hung up their spikes, but the flying Dutchwoman produced a parade of peak performances that earned her four gold medals and a permanent place in Olympic history as one of the greatest women competitors of all time.

Born in Amsterdam in the last year of the First World War, Francina Koen was encouraged to take up athletics by her father after she had revealed all-round sporting talent at school. She used to make a thirty-mile round trip every day by bicycle to train under the guidance of Jan Blankers, an outstanding triple jumper who won the AAA title in London in 1931 and again in 1933. Jan married Fanny in 1940, and continued to coach her. He motivated her for the London Olympics with the deliberate taunt: 'They are saying you are too old, Fanny. Go out and prove them wrong.' Since the Berlin Games, she had set or equalled world records in the 100 yards, 100 metres, long jump, high jump and 80 metres hurdles.

Fanny Blankers-Koen: the 'Flying Dutchwoman'

VALERI BORZOV
USSR (1949)

Cynics claim that Valeri Borzov was the first Olympic champion created by a computer. They are being less than fair to a great sprinter who had natural style and grace to go with his lightning speed. Ukraine-born Borzov was the product of an intensive search by Soviet coaches for an athlete to end the supremacy of the United States in the sprint events. A team of physiologists and coaches headed by Professor Valentin Petrovsky fed all the attributes for the 'perfect' sprinter into a computer and then proceeded to programme Borzov to meet the requirements. It was a merger of the world of athletics and that of science but Borzov, while clearly benefiting from technical advice during his training preparation in Kiev, had to have the talent to succeed in the first place.

He had a remarkable record of consistency from the moment he burst into international prominence when winning the European junior 100 and 200 metre titles in 1968. He followed this five months later by equalling the world indoor best of 6.4 sec for 60 metres and then, in 1969, he equalled the outdoor

Valeri Borzov: the rocketman from the Ukraine

The hardest job was deciding which events to enter in the 1948 Olympics. She settled for the 100 metres, 200 metres and 80 metres hurdles, and she proceeded to win them all over an electrifying span of just nine days during which she competed 12 times in heats and finals and broke the tape in every race. She then completed her gold rush by anchoring the Dutch sprint relay team to victory, taking over the baton in third place and overhauling the leaders with an inspired burst in the last 20 metres. Three British girls won silver medals behind Fanny — Dorothy Manley (100m), Audrey Williamson (200m) and Maureen Gardner (80m hurdles).

She was homesick and missed her children so much during the London Games that she considered retirement, but the call of the track was too strong. During the next four years she set a new world record for 220 yards, won three titles in the European championships in Brussels and then switched to the pentathlon and created a new world record of 4692 points. A blood infection prevented her producing winning form in the 1952 Helsinki Olympics and she bowed out of competitive athletics as the first lady of the track, continuing to serve her sport in an administrative capacity.

European record of 10.0 sec for 100 metres. His victories in the senior European championships in 1969 and 1971 underlined the fact that the Russians had discovered a truly world-class sprinter ready for the 1972 Olympics in Munich.

A feature of his running was a rocket start and a silky smoothness when in full stride that made it look as if he was running at less than full throttle. He effortlessly won the 100 metres title in Munich in 10.14 sec, and then he had to ride the taunts that his victory was an empty one because the two leading American challengers had not competed. They had been barred after failing to turn up in time for the quarter-finals. Borzov silenced the doubters with a magnificent run in the 200 metres final, going through the tape with both hands raised in triumph and with the clock stopped at a European record 20.00 sec. The victory made him the first European ever to win the men's Olympic sprint double.

His only defeat in a major championship came in the 100 metres final in the 1976 Olympics. He finished third, again in 10.14 sec, and so became the first Olympic 100 metres champion to collect a second medal in the same event. Borzov set his sights on representing the USSR in the 1980 Games in Moscow but a recurring Achilles tendon injury forced his retirement. In what was described as 'the sporting union of the century', Borzov married Russia's great Olympic gymnastics champion Ludmilla Turischeva. The mind boggles at the thought of what their offspring could produce if they inherit a combination of the ability with which their famous parents were blessed.

RALPH BOSTON
United States (1939)
Until Bob Beamon's sensational take-off in the 1968 Games in Mexico, Ralph Boston was renowned and respected as the great barrier-breaker in the long jump. He was the man who finally removed Jesse Owens' 25-year-old world record from the books and in 1961 he became the first long-jumper to clear 27 feet (8.23 m). Boston, born in Mississippi, increased the world record six times before Beamon's boomer. In the course of a distinguished nine-year international career he completed a full set of Olympic medals. He won the gold in 1960, a silver behind Britain's Lynn Davies in 1964, and a bronze in Mexico after he had watched Beamon wipe out all opposition with his historic 29ft 2½in leap into the land of Olympic legend.

The youngest of ten children, he started long-jumping at the age of fourteen, and earned an athletics scholarship to Tennessee State University where he developed into a magnificent all-rounder. He was an outstanding sprinter and was also near world class as a high-jumper, pole-vaulter and hurdler. But it was the long jump that claimed his main attention and in terms of high-level consistency

there has never been anybody to touch him. This universally popular competitor retired after the 1968 Olympics to concentrate on a new career as an athletics commentator.

ALBERTO BRAGLIA
Italy (1883-1954)
Considered the 'father' of Italian gymnastics, Alberto Braglia won gold medals in the combined exercises at the 1908 Olympics in London and in the 1912 Games in Stockholm. He had first come to international prominence in the 1906 Interim Olympics in Athens when he finished joint champion in the pentathlon and hexathlon events. Braglia was a superb all-rounder who set new standards of technical precision and he had the sense of balance of a high-wire walker. His greatest contribution to his sport came after his retirement when he passed on his technique to a procession of gymnasts as a world-renowned coach. He was in charge of the Italian team that collected four gymnastic gold medals in the 1932 Games in Los Angeles and he remained a sporting idol in Italy right up until his death in 1954.

CHRIS BRASHER
Great Britain (1928)
Chris Brasher has become best known as the man who brought the fun and the festival of the people's marathon to London but it was as an athlete in his own right that he first earned international fame. He was a capable rather than outstanding middle-distance runner for most of his career, yet proved that by a mixture of determination, discipline and perseverance even an 'ordinary' athlete could conquer the world. Brasher, a Cambridge University graduate, brought his single-minded attitude as an expert mountaineer to the track and refused to concede that an Olympic medal was beyond his reach.

His chief distinction before the 1956 Games in Melbourne was that he had joined Chris Chataway in pacing Roger Bannister to the first sub-four-minute mile at Oxford in 1954. It was in the 3000 metres steeplechase that he found the most suitable outlet for the strength and stamina he had accumulated in his many mountain assaults. He finished 11th out of 12 in the final of the steeplechase in the 1952 Helsinki Olympics. It was a run that captured his great courage and character because he was carrying an injury that would have forced most men out of the race. He went to Melbourne as England's late-choice third string in the steeplechase and was not considered in with a hope of a medal. Brasher, however, was quietly confident even though he had never won a national title or any major international event of any consequence. He ran the race of a lifetime in the 1956 final to break the tape in an Olympic record 8 min 41.2 sec. His nearest rival finished 15 metres behind but Brasher's celebration at being Britain's first Olympic track gold medallist for twenty-four years was cut short by the devastating announcement that he had been disqualified. It was alleged that he had obstructed an opponent on the last lap but he was reinstated as champion some two and a half hours later after the jury of appeal had held an investigation. Born to British parents in Georgetown, Guyana, Brasher retired after his Olympic triumph and went on to new successes as a journalist with the *Observer*, a television broadcaster, a pioneer of British orienteering and, of course, an organizer of marathons.

VALERI BRUMEL
USSR (1942)

This remarkable Russian had virtually *two* careers as a high-jumper, the first ended by a leg injury that literally crippled him for more than three years after he had established himself as the world's No 1 in his event. His right shin bone was shattered in a motorcycle accident in Moscow in October, 1965. A year earlier he had won the Olympic gold medal in Tokyo to add to the silver he had collected in Rome four years before. At the time of the accident he was the world record holder at 7ft 5¾in, a height that remained unconquered for eight years. It was an astonishing leap, not only in terms of the elevation but because the bar was seventeen inches above his own height. Surgeons sadly shook their heads and agreed there was no way that Brumel could continue his career following the accident. Six major operations left him with the damaged right leg nearly two inches shorter than the left, and he was unable to walk without the aid of crutches. Brumel was convinced he would compete again and in 1968 he returned to his home region of Siberia for revolutionary treatment during which his leg was stretched back to its natural length. He made what was a miraculous comeback in 1969, and while unable to reach the heights of his former glory, he was an advertisement for courage and the wonders of medical science.

Brumel had started high-jumping at the age of eleven, but it was not until 1960 that he came to world prominence with an astonishing 7½in improvement during a single athletics season. Using the straddle technique, he raised the outdoor world record six times between 1961 and 1963 and was also the world's No 1 on the indoors circuit until the accident that sidelined him for what were expected to be his peak years as a competitor.

LORD DAVID BURGHLEY
Great Britain (1905-1981)

It was fitting that when David Hemery won the 400 metres hurdles in the 1968 Mexico Olympics he was presented with his gold medal by Lord Burghley, who won the event for Britain forty years earlier. Few people have been able to match Lord David Burghley's contribution to athletics, first as an exceptional hurdler and later as a home and international administrator who had drive, enthusiasm and great vision. Educated at Eton and Cambridge, he made his Olympic debut in the 110 metres hurdles in Paris in 1920 and suffered the disappointment of being eliminated in the first round. Four years later in Amsterdam he became the first man to break the American domination in the 400 metres hurdles, leading from gun to tape in the final and clocking an Olympic record 53.4sec. He went into politics after his triumph and became a Member of Parliament but remained heavily involved in athletics. Captain of the England team in the first Empire Games of 1930, he collected gold medals in the 120 and 440 yards hurdles and also in the 4 x 440 yards relay.

He reached the finals of both the 110 and 400 metres hurdles in the 1932 Los Angeles Olympics but the best he could manage was fourth place in the longer event in which he set a new British record of 52.3 sec. The gold medal went to his former Cambridge University team-mate Bob Tisdall of Ireland. Lord Burghley — later the sixth Marquess of Exeter — had the consolation of picking up a silver medal as a member of Britain's 4 x 400 metres relay team. Nicknamed 'His Hurdling Lordship', he retired in 1933 after losing his AAA 440 yards hurdles title to his great Italian rival Luigi Facelli. His name remained in the British record books for a span of twenty-five years before the times he had set in the 1920s were toppled. Lord Burghley was President of the AAA for forty years and of the International Amateur Athletic Federation from 1946 until 1976. He continued his close ties with the Olympics by becoming a member of the International Olympic Committee in 1933.

MIKE BURTON
United States (1947)

Mike Burton's dream of becoming a top athlete died when at the age of thirteen he was knocked off his bike by a truck. One of his legs was so severely injured that doctors doubted whether he would walk again without the aid of crutches. He was advised to take up swimming to help rebuild the leg muscles. Eight years later he splashed through the water at the Mexico Olympics to take the gold medals in both the 400 metres and 1500 metres, breaking the Olympic records in both events. Nicknamed 'The Machine' because of his incredible training output under the guidance of coach Sherman Chavoor, he continually lowered the world records for the 800 and 1500 metres and retained his Olympic title over the longer distance with a world record swim in Munich in 1972. Burton, who became a respected swimming coach and a member of the US Olympic Committee, was the first man to win the 1500 metres freestyle title at two successive Games.

LEE CALHOUN
United States (1933)

Lee Calhoun, born in the same small Mississippi town of Laurel as long-jumper Ralph Boston, was never far from drama during his career as one of the greatest of all high hurdlers. He dead heated with Jack Davis for first place in the 1956 Olympic US trials and six weeks later was judged to have beaten Davis by the thickness of an athletics vest in the Olympic 110 metres hurdles final in Melbourne. Two years later Calhoun was suspended from athletics for allegedly cashing in on his Olympic fame by entering a 'Bride and Groom' television quiz show with his wife and receiving gifts that included a swimming pool and a honeymoon trip to Paris. He was forgiven and reinstated after making a gift of the swimming pool to a youth club and in his comeback season equalled the world 110 metres hurdles record of 13.2 sec. Using a spectacular dip-finish technique to beat countryman Willie May by two-hundredths of a second in the 1960 Rome Games, Calhoun became the first man to retain an Olympic high hurdles title. He started his athletics career as a high-jumper but switched to hurdling under the influence of 1952 Olympic high hurdles champion Harrison Dillard.

VERA CASLAVSKA
Czechoslovakia (1942)

Lithe and lovely Vera Caslavska did more than anybody to popularize gymnastics with her stunning performances in the 1968 Olympics in Mexico. The winner of five world championships in 1965 and 1967, she went to Mexico as the reigning Olympic champion in three events and proceeded to add four gold medals to her glittering collection. She captured the imagination of millions of television viewers who warmed not only to her grace and beauty but also to her courage. Vera produced almost faultless performances in Mexico City barely two months after having gone into hiding in her home-town of Prague following the invasion of Czechoslovakia by Russian troops. Her fitness programme was seriously disrupted and her only physical activity in the weeks leading up to her departure for Mexico was humping sacks of coal.

Spurred on by the knowledge that beating Russian opponents would boost morale at home, Vera was in inspired form in the Olympics and she won gold medals for the combined exercises, horse vault and asymmetric bars, was joint first in the floor exercises and gained silver medals in the beam and team event. The beautiful blonde Czech, who had concentrated on ice skating and ballet until switching to gymnastics at fifteen, was the heroine of Mexico and completely won over the hosts when she selected the

Vera Caslavska: captured the imagination and 11 medals

'Mexican Hat Dance' as the background music for her floor exercise routine.

Vera brought romance to the Games just a few days after her triumph in the gymnasium when she married Czech 1500 metres runner Josef Odlozil at the Roman Catholic cathedral in the centre of Mexico City. On her return home she presented her four gold medals to four Czech leaders who had defied the Russian regime. Her total haul of Olympic medals — seven gold and four silver — made her the most successful woman competitor in Olympic history.

DHYAN CHAND
India (1905)

Dhyan Chand was 'The Master' of the hockey field and there has rarely, if ever, been a player in the game to compare with him for all-round skill, stick-control and finishing finesse. He was to hockey what Pele was to football and Bradman was to cricket. Chand followed his father and an elder brother into the Army at the age of sixteen and began to learn how to play hockey from the British officers. The pupil was soon showing his masters how the game could be played and astonished them with his ball-juggling tricks. He played centre-forward in the Indian teams which won the Olympic gold medal in 1928 and 1932 and he was captain of the side that completed the hat-trick with a memorable victory over Germany in the 1936 final in Berlin. The German favourites were confident they could win with the game evenly balanced at half-time but then Chand revealed the full range of his skill and scored six times as India romped to an 8-1 victory.

In the three Olympic tournaments India amassed a total of 102 goals and conceded just three. Chand, who was promoted after each triumph, finished up as a major and with a reputation as a genius of a hockey player that has never dimmed with the passing years. During a tour of New Zealand in 1935 he scored 201 goals out of an aggregate of 584. India's second most successful marksman was Chand's brother Roopsingh. Dhyan retired in 1948 and became coach to the national team.

VIKTOR CHUKARIN
USSR (1921)

It was Viktor Chukarin who first revealed Russia's emergence as a world power in the gymnasium. The agile Ukrainian collected seven gold medals in the Olympics of 1952 and 1956 and set new standards of perfection on the parallel bars. He more than anybody inspired the explosion of talent in the Soviet Union that has survived through generations of outstanding gymnasts. Chukarin led the first Russian team to compete in an Olympic gymnastics tournament in 1952 and took the coveted individual gold medal in the combined exercises. He retained the Olympic title in Melbourne two years after sharing

the world championship with compatriot Valentin Muratov. As well as his seven golds, this master of the gymnasium also won three silvers and a bronze.

WALDEMAR CIERPINSKI
East Germany (1950)

Few people gave Waldemar Cierpinski a chance of challenging for the gold medal in the 1976 Olympic marathon in Montreal. He was best known on the international circuit as a steeplechaser and his four previous marathon outings had produced little to suggest he could beat the cream of the world's distance runners. However, with typical East German thoroughness he had been installed in the Olympic Village three weeks before any of his rivals, and his meticulous, painstaking preparations for the race ensured his 'peaking' at just the right time. Defending champion Frank Shorter forced the pace from the early stages, along with his highly regarded United States team-mate Bill Rodgers, Canadian Jerome Drayton, 1972 Olympic silver medallist Karel Lismont and 5000 and 10,000 metres gold medallist

Waldemar Cierpinski: hoping for a historic hat-trick

Lasse Viren, who was making his marathon debut in a bid to repeat Emil Zatopek's remarkable hat-trick of 1952. Cierpinski kept with this leading bunch for 30 km and then, just when he was expected to crack, increased the tempo until he had literally run out of rivals. He stretched his lead over second man Shorter to 50 seconds and, looking remarkably fresh in driving rain, crossed the finishing-line in an Olympic record of 2 hr 9 min 55 sec, two and a half minutes faster than he had ever run before.

Cierpinski was dismissed as a one-race wonder by many people following a series of unimpressive performances over the next four years. But he and his coach Walter Schmidt had only one target in mind — a second Olympic gold medal in the 1980 Games. He retained his title in Moscow with a composed, almost mechanical performance, keeping a disciplined pace rather than chase after runaway Mexican leader Rodolfo Gomez, who was at one stage nearly half a minute ahead of the defending champion. Cierpinski gradually brought Gomez into his sights and then, as in Montreal, gave a little touch to the accelerator to move smoothly into the lead. He finished a convincing winner in 2 hr 11min 03 sec to join the legendary

Abebe Bikila as the only man to win two Olympic marathons.

There was conjecture whether 'sports student' Cierpinski — two days off his thirtieth birthday — would have triumphed had the Americans and Japanese not boycotted the Games. But he won when it mattered against a lot of tough opposition, and the eyes of the world will be trained on him when he bids for a historic hat-trick in Los Angeles.

CASSIUS CLAY
United States (1942)

The world's most famous chatter-boxer first came to international prominence in the 1960 Rome Olympics when answering to what he later claimed was his 'slave' name, Cassius Marcellus Clay. Competing as a 12 st 6 lb light-heavyweight, Clay gave glimpses of the ring magic that was to make him a legend in his own lifetime. His most powerful weapon was a stabbing left jab that he used to excellent effect in the

Cassius Clay: the chatterboxer on the winner's rostrum

final when outpointing Poland's accomplished European champion Zbigniew Pietrzykowski.

Clay, 'The Louisville Lip' from Kentucky, was so proud of his Olympic medal that he slept with it around his neck on the night of his triumph. Some fifteen years later he confessed that he had thrown the medal into the Ohio river soon after his return to the United States after he had been refused service in a coffee bar because he was black. Clay took the world professional heavyweight championship from Sonny Liston in 1964 and then announced that he was changing his name to Muhammad Ali. But it is as 'Gaseous Cassius' Clay that he will always be remembered as an Olympic hero.

NADIA COMANECI
Romania (1962)

Nadia Comaneci, a fourteen-year-old Romanian schoolgirl, became the heroine of the 1976 Montreal Olympics with a history-making exhibition of sheer perfection in the gymnasium. She was awarded maximum points for her performances on the beam and asymmetric bars, the first perfect ten-out-of-ten

Nadia Comaneci: the ballerina of the bars

points total in Olympic competition. Nadia, though lacking the charismatic magnetism of 1972 wondergirl Olga Korbut, was in a class of her own for technique and skill and her individual display dampened Russia's victory in the team event.

Her arrival as a world star was incredibly swift. Less than two years earlier she had failed to win a place in the Romanian team for the world championships. She had made such rapid improvement by the time of the Olympics that she dropped only 0.30 points over the four pieces of apparatus — an incredible consistency that was without parallel in the sport. Despite strong competition from a powerful Russian challenge led by Nelli Kim, Ludmilla Turischeva and Olga Korbut, Nadia was the all-round women's champion as well as taking two individual golds and a silver in the team event.

Nadia was taller and heavier by the time of the 1980 Games in Moscow but she had lost none of her grace, and again scored a perfect '10' on the beam, in which event she took the individual gold medal. She shared another gold with nimble Nelli Kim in the floor exercises. The Moscow gymnastics were soured by angry disputes over the marking by the judges and Nadia was twice the victim of controversial scores. She had to be satisfied with a joint silver medal in the combined exercises and had to surrender the asymmetric title she won in such style in Montreal when she fell off during her voluntary routine.

HAL CONNOLLY
United States (1931)

Harold (Hal) Connolly has had the sort of experiences you would expect to exist only in the fertile imagination of a Hollywood script-writer. A withered left arm, three inches shorter than his right, seemed to rule him out from making any great sporting impact yet he established himself as one of the greatest competitors in the history of hammer-throwing. He became the first American to beat the magic 200 foot mark in 1955, and the following year won the Olympic title in Melbourne and set the first of seven world records in the event.

However, the biggest headlines in Melbourne were reserved for his private life. The 25-year-old Boston school-teacher met and fell in love with 23-year-old Czech discus champion Olga Fikotova during training at the Olympic Village. Olga won a gold medal and, more important, she also won Hal's heart. It was a barrier-breaking romance that captured the interest and imagination of millions of people around the world and the couple battled through miles of political red tape to conquer Czech resistance to their planned marriage. One of the most publicized sporting weddings of all time finally took place in Prague on 27 March 1957, with legendary Czech runner Emil Zatopek as best man and his wife, Dana, as the matron of honour.

Happy Hal took his beautiful bride home to

Hal Connolly: won a gold medal and a bride

California, where they continued to concentrate on their athletics. They competed together in the next three Olympics but without managing to repeat their 1956 victories. 'Each Olympics is like a honeymoon for us,' said Hal, who was born of Irish stock and revived the old Irish-American dominance in the hammer.

He spotlighted the darker side of athletics during an investigation into drug-taking when he told a US Senate Committee in 1973: 'For eight years prior to 1972 I would have to refer to myself as a hooked athlete. Like all my rivals, I was using anabolic steroids as an integral part of my training. I knew any number of athletes in the 1968 Olympic team who had so much scar tissue and so many puncture holes on their backsides that it was difficult to find a fresh spot to give them a new shot. I relate these incidents to emphasize my contention that the overwhelming majority of the international track and field athletes I know would take anything and do anything to improve their athletic performances.'

Olga, who has established herself as a respected writer in the United States, became heavily involved — along with her husband — in the civil rights movement in sport. She also found time to bring up four children, including twins, and twelve years after her gold-medal winning performance in Melbourne this former Czech basketball international managed

to produce a lifetime's best discus throw of 178ft 5in. There is no 'they lived happily ever after' ending to this story because Hal has since married former Olympic pentathlete Pat Winslow, who coaches top US sprinter Evelyn Ashford.

ADOLFO CONSOLINI
Italy (1917-1969)
Europe has rarely had a discus-thrower to match Adolfo Consolini for sheer consistency. The 6ft, 16-stone Goliath made his debut in the event at the age of nineteen in 1937 and was still competing at the highest level nearly twenty-five years later. He broke the world record with a throw of 175ft in 1941 and had his greatest triumph in the London Olympics of 1948 when he won the gold medal after a terrific tussle with his countryman Giuseppe Tosi, each of them beating the old Olympic record. Two months later Consolini increased the world record to 181ft 6½in. He was Olympic silver medallist in 1952, just four feet behind Sim Iness of the United States. The popular veteran finished sixth in the Melbourne Games in 1956 and seventeenth in Rome four years later at the age of forty-three. From the time when he won his first Italian title in 1940 with a throw of just over 165 feet, Consolini was virtually unbeatable against European opposition. He won nineteen Italian championships and was three times European title-holder. The Italian idol was rarely below 50

metres (164ft) with any throw in a run of more than 350 competitions and had a lifetime's best of 186ft 11¾in in 1955, a European record that stood for four years.

LORRAINE CRAPP
Australia (1938)
Australian freestyler Lorraine Crapp distinguished herself in August 1956 by becoming the first woman to break the five-minute barrier for 400 metres, which was considered the swimming equivalent of Roger Bannister's four-minute-mile run two years earlier. On the way to her history-making record she set new world best times for the 200 metres and 220 yards and also beat the 440 yards record. Two months later she lowered the four records again when clocking an astonishing 4 min 47.2 sec for the 400 metres. Needless to say she won the gold medal in the 400 metres in the Melbourne Olympics the following month, collected another gold in the 4 x 100 metres relay and finished second behind another great Australian mermaid, Dawn Fraser, in the 100 metres.

Just a year before this record-breaking spree, Lorraine had been forced to consider retiring from competitive swimming because of a severe ear infection. She overcame the problem, however, and continued competing in international events until the 1960 Olympics, in which she won a silver medal as a member of the Australian 4 x 100 metres relay team. Coached by Frank Guthrie, Lorraine first came to world prominence when setting world records for the 800 metres and 880 yards in January, 1954. In the same year she won gold medals in the 110 yards and 440 yards freestyle events in the Empire Games in Vancouver. In all, she achieved or shared in sixteen world records during a glittering career that set new standards for women swimmers.

BETTY CUTHBERT
Australia (1938)
Betty Cuthbert — the 'Blonde Beaut' of Australian athletics — spurted to international fame with a triple-gold streak in the 1956 Melbourne Olympics in front of her own adoring fans who worshipped the ground she ran on. She won the 100 metres in 11.5 sec after setting an Olympic record of 11.4 sec in the heats. Then she took the gold medal in the 200 metres with an Olympic-record-equalling time of 23.4sec. In each final her nearest rival was two metres behind at the tape. Hurricane Betty completed her domination of the Melbourne sprints by anchoring Australia to a 4 x 100 metres relay victory in a world record 44.5 sec.

Yet only a year earlier she had not been rated in the world's top twenty sprinters. A twin who was born at Merrylands, New South Wales, Betty had been forced to race in the shadow of her compatriot Marlene Matthews in the two years leading up to the 1956 Olympics. But she 'peaked' at just the right time

and emerged as the eighteen-year-old heroine of the Melbourne Games. To cap a memorable year, she shared in three world relay records during a match between the British Commonwealth and the United States immediately following the Olympics.

Betty, coached by 1948 Olympic relay silver medallist June Masters (later Mrs Ferguson), suffered an enormous anti-climax after her golden hat-trick in Melbourne and found it difficult to handle the sudden rush of fame. She set world records for 220 yards and 440 yards, yet failed to make any real impact in the major championships. A hamstring injury prevented her defending her titles in the 1960 Rome Olympics but she regained all her old appetite and sharpness in time for the Tokyo Games of 1964, by which time she had stepped up to the 400 metres. She shook off the handicap of a foot injury to get herself in peak condition for the final, in which she judged her finish to perfection to beat Britain's Ann Packer in 52 sec. It made her the first woman athlete since Fanny Blankers-Koen to win four Olympic gold medals on the track.

LYNN DAVIES
Great Britain (1942)
Lynn (The Leap) Davies is arguably the greatest competitive athlete ever to wear a British international vest. A magnificent all-rounder who specialized in the long jump, he holds the unique record of being the only athlete to complete a 'grand slam' collection of gold medals in the Olympic, European and Commonwealth championships. He experienced the most satisfying moment of his marvellous career in the 1964 Tokyo Games when he became the first Welsh Olympic champion and Britain's first Olympic gold medallist in the field events since 1908.

He went to Tokyo to challenge for the long-jump title with little real hope of a gold medal. His rivals included world record holder Ralph Boston, the defending champion who had consistently beaten Lynn's best mark of 26 ft 4 in and had produced a near-28ft wind-assisted leap just a month before the Games. Also in the field was Russian Igor Ter-Ovanesyan, one of the all-time-great long-jumpers who many people considered would be the first man to beat the 28 ft barrier. Davies, using the two-and-a-half hitchkick technique that his coach Ron Pickering had helped him perfect during the previous year, qualified for the final with his last jump in the preliminary round.

The weather was atrocious for the final. The runway was soaking wet and the rain and a biting cold wind was hitting the jumpers in the face. 'It's just like home,' Lynn said with a tight smile before going to the runway for the fifth jump that was to prove the leap of a lifetime. He called on all the competitive qualities that have made him such a respected figure in the world of sport and unleashed a British record jump of 26 ft 5.3/4in (8.07 m). It was an astonishing performance considering the alien conditions and even the bounding Boston could not beat it, finishing with a best effort of 26 ft 4 in (8.03m).

Davies, born in Nant-y-Moel, had started out as a triple jumper but switched to the long jump after a succession of injuries. He added the European and Commonwealth titles to his honours haul in 1966 and went to Mexico to defend his Olympic crown in 1968 in a mood of confidence after beating the 27-foot barrier for the first time. It was in Mexico, of course, that Bob Beamon produced his prodigious 29 ft leap and deflated Davies in the process. Lynn collected a silver medal in the 1969 European championships, had the satisfaction of beating Beamon in a non-championship event in Stuttgart and retained his Commonwealth title in 1970. Injury prevented him making more than a token challenge for the Olympic crown in 1972, and he retired to take up a position as technical director of Canadian athletics. He returned home to manage the British athletics team in the 1980 Moscow Games, and gave further evidence of his great all-round ability with a succession of fine performances in the TV Superstars series. Even when he was past forty he proved a model athlete, with a fine physique and above all a competitive attitude.

GLENN DAVIS
United States (1934)
Nicknamed 'Jeep' because of his stamina and all-round ability, Glenn Davis achieved the astonishing distinction of winning the 1956 Olympic 400 metres hurdles gold medal in his first season of taking up the event. He was such an outstanding all-rounder that he once won an inter-schools athletics meet as a one-man team! It was not until the spring of 1956 that he decided to concentrate on the 'killer' one-lap hurdles event and within six months he won the Olympic title in 50.1 sec after setting a world record at 49.5 sec in the US Olympic trials. Davis, born in Wellsburg, West Virginia, created Olympic history four years later by becoming the first hurdler to retain the 400 metres title, his winning time of 49.3 sec being only one-tenth of a second outside his 1958 world record. He made it a hat-trick of gold medals when he ran the third leg for America's winning 4 x 400 metres relay team. His all-round strength is revealed in these career-best figures: 100 metres (10.3 sec), 200 metres (21.0 sec), 440 yards (45.7 sec in 1958 — then a world record), 200 metres hurdles (22.5 sec, a world record), long jump (24ft 0¼in), high jump (6ft 3½in).

JOHN DAVIS
United States (1921)
Prison warder John Davis had little trouble earning the respect of the inmates. The moustachioed, heavily muscled black American proved himself one of the strongest men in the world during a weight-lifting career that spanned sixteen years from when

he won his first world title at the age of seventeen in 1938. Davis, winner of the Olympic heavyweight title in 1948 and again in 1952, was the first man to snatch 300 lb in competition and the first to beat the 400 lb barrier in the clean-and-jerk. Scaling just a few pounds over 15 stone, Davis was not huge by modern weight-lifting standards but he had enormous power — particularly in his legs, as he demonstrated by unofficially beating the standing long-jump world record during an exhibition while training.

Virtually unbeatable in the immediate post-war years, Davis had a modest, unassuming nature that made him popular among his rivals. The nearest he came to defeat in a major championship during his peak years was in 1951 when he injured a leg while defending his world title in Milan. It left the way open for his team-mate Jim Bradford to beat him but he declined to attempt a winning lift. 'John is the rightful king,' said true sportsman Bradford. 'It would not be right to beat him like this.' Davis was finally dethroned as world champion in 1953 when he had to bow to the superiority of club-footed Canadian Doug Hepburn, who outweighed the legendary American strongman by six stone and launched a new era of super-heavyweight weight-lifters.

RONNIE DELANY
Republic of Ireland (1935)
The Irish selectors dithered over whether to send Ronnie Delany to the 1956 Olympics in Melbourne to compete in the 1500 metres after a disappointing season in which he had twice been comprehensively beaten by England's Brian Hewson. He had become the seventh man in history to duck under four minutes for the mile in Compton, California, early in 1956, but his form deserted him on his return to Ireland where the Olympic selectors looked on aghast as he struggled through a mile race in 4 min 20 sec. He went back to America to continue his studies at Villanova University and to step up his training under coach Jim 'Jumbo' Elliott, hoping that the selectors would take his early form into consideration when picking their team. It was not until the eve of the Olympics that he heard that he had, almost reluctantly, been picked.

He qualified quietly for the 1500 metres final, finishing third in his heat, and few people saw him as anything of a threat to the race favourites who included top Europeans Brian Hewson, Laszlo Tabori (Hungary), Stanislav Jungwirth (Czechoslovakia) and Klaus Richtzenhain (West Germany). Australasia was also powerfully represented by Murray Halberg, Merv Lincoln and the redoubtable John Landy. Delany was tucked back in tenth place as the bell signalled the last lap of the final and there seemed no way he could force himself into the reckoning for a medal. However, the finishing instinct he had sharpened in dozens of races on the boards during the American indoor season was suddenly brought into play. He picked off one runner after another and his green vest was almost a blur as he came flying off the final bend to take the lead and then break the tape with his arms spread wide in triumph. He was nearly four metres ahead of silver medallist Richtzenhain and had covered the last lap in a breath-taking 54 seconds.

Delany, born in Arklow, Co Wicklow, lowered his best mile time to 3 min 58.8 sec the following year when finishing second in Derek Ibbotson's world record run of 3 min 57.2 sec at London's White City. Then he brought it down to 3 min 57.7 sec in Dublin in 1958, this time when coming home third in Herb Elliott's world record run of 3 min 54.5 sec. But the likeable Irishman won in the race that *really* mattered.

PETE DESJARDINS
United States (1908)
French-Canadian by birth but a naturalized citizen of the United States, Pete Desjardins became during the 1928 Games the only diver in Olympic history to earn maximum points. The man known as 'The Little Bronze Statue' touched perfection in the three-metre springboard competition, twice gettting ten-out-of-ten ratings from the judges to clinch a gold medal to go with the silver he had won four years earlier. Desjardins, who had a perfectly sculptured 5 ft 3 in frame, completed the double when he won the highboard title. Born in Manitoba and raised in Miami, he studied economics at Stanford University before turning professional and touring the world, giving diving exhibitions that drew massive crowds wherever he performed.

KLAUS DIBIASI
Italy (1947)
Klaus Dibiasi, born in Austria of Italian parents, completed a historic hat-trick in the 1976 Games in Montreal when he became the first diver to win three successive Olympic highboard titles. He had started his medal-collection in the 1964 Olympics, when at the age of seventeen he took the silver in the highboard event. His success in Tokyo was greeted with such enthusiasm in his home-town of Bolzano that a public fund was started to help build a special diving pool so that he could train locally throughout the year. He won the gold in the highboard diving and the springboard silver in Mexico in 1968 and retained his highboard title in Munich four years later.

Coached by his father — a former Italian springboard diving champion — Dibiasi insisted on going through with a second defence of his Olympic title in Montreal despite suffering from tendonitis in both heels. He was given tough competition by Californian Greg Louganis but clinched his record third title with a remarkable fifth dive — a triple twist with one and a half somersaults — that brought applause even from his rivals.

Klaus Dibiasi: a hat-trick on the highboard

MILDRED DIDRIKSON
United States (1914-1956)
There has never been an all-round sportswoman quite like Mildred 'Babe' Didrikson. There will be particularly warm memories of her during the 1984 Games in the Olympic Stadium in Los Angeles because it was in that same arena in 1932 that she confirmed her standing as one of the greatest women athletes of all time. She won the 80 metres hurdles in a world record 11.7 sec, won the javelin gold medal with another world record and had a possible gold medal in the high jump cruelly snatched from her because the judges ruled that her dive-and-roll technique was illegal. She and her American team-mate Jean Shiley had tied at a world record equalling height of 5ft 5¼in and they had both gone clear in a

Mildred 'Babe' Didrikson: nobody quite like her

centrefield to the plate, played international-class lacrosse, was an expert at diving and billiards and was twice selected for the All-American basketball team. She made headlines in her private life when she married gigantic professional wrestler George Zaharias, who weighed in at 285 lb and was billed as 'The Crying Greek from Cripple Creek.'

In 1950, Babe was voted woman athlete of the half-century in a poll organized by the Associated Press. She toured in a vaudeville act in which she gave demonstrations of her sporting prowess, and for good measure also played the harmonica. It was on the professional golf circuit that she gained the greatest respect, often beating top male opponents in head-to-head clashes. She won four successive women's world golf championships and continued to tour the golf circuit until shortly before her death from cancer at the age of forty-two in 1956. There will never be another quite like her.

HARRISON DILLARD
United States (1923)

A thirteen-year-old Cleveland, Ohio, schoolboy called Harrison Dillard was so inspired by a cinema newsreel report of the golden exploits of Jesse Owens in the 1936 Berlin Olympics that he vowed that he would one day emulate his hero. Jesse Owens got to hear about it, and he gave Dillard his Olympic running shoes to help further fuel his ambition. Dillard provided action to go with his words and while a student at Ohio's Baldwin-Wallace College established himself as the greatest high hurdler in the world. An Olympic gold medal seemed his for the taking in the 1948 Games in London after a streak of 82 races without defeat between May 1947 and June 1948. But Dillard's golden dreams became a nightmare in the US Olympic trials when his trailing leg hit a hurdle and he crashed to the track. There are no second chances in American athletics. You either finish in the first three in the Olympic trials or you don't get invited to the Games. Dillard buried his deep disappointment and switched his concentration to the 100 metres, scraping through to the squad for London with a third place behind world record holders Mel Patton and Barney Ewell.

Dillard — nicknamed Bones because of his slim, rubber-like physique — rushed to a shock gold medal victory in the 100 metres final at Wembley, and as he sliced through the tape the clock stopped at 10.3 sec to equal the Olympic record set by his idol Jesse Owens in Berlin. He then helped the United States squad take the gold in the 4 x 100 metres sprint relay. Four years later Dillard made no mistakes in his favourite hurdles event in which he was the world record holder. He pipped team-mate Jack Davis in the 110 metres hurdles final, both finishing in a new Olympic record 13.7 sec. Dillard added a fourth gold medal to his collection as a member of the winning sprint relay quartet.

jump-off when the judges made their shattering decision. Mildred, who had been using the same jumping technique all afternoon, was allowed to collect the silver medal.

She was nicknamed 'Babe' when she first established herself as a world-class athlete while still at school in Port Arthur, Texas, where she was born in 1914 of Norwegian parents. Mildred set a world record in the javelin at the age of sixteen and two years later, just before the 1932 Olympics, produced an astonishing one-girl show when she won the US women's national team athletics championship on her own. She finished first in five events and was placed in three more in one afternoon's competition. The team that came second in the overall championship had twenty-two competitors!

Babe was barred from amateur athletics shortly after her triumph in the 1932 Games because she lent her name to an advertising campaign for automobiles, but her all-round sporting career was only just taking off. She took up golf and won seventeen national titles between 1934 and 1950. The girl with the golden charm also hit three baseball home runs in one game, made a remarkable 313 ft throw from the

PIERO (1923) and
RAIMONDO (1925) D'INZEO
(Italy)

The sons of a riding instructor in the Italian Army, Piero and Raimondo were born to ride and became giants of the show-jumping world. Piero followed his father into the army as well as the saddle. Raimondo studied at Rome University before joining the Italian cavalry and then the *carabinieri* where his passion for horses could be satisfied. Both brothers made their Olympic debuts in 1948 but it was not until the 1956 Games — staged in Stockholm — that they proved themselves truly world class. Raimondo took the individual silver medal, Piero the bronze and Italy the team silver. That same year Raimondo won the world championship, a title he retained in 1960. Piero was European champion in 1959.

The d'Inzeo brothers enjoyed the greatest moments of their long, distinguished careers on home territory in the 1960 Rome Olympics. Raimondo took the individual gold, Piero the silver and their brilliant riding lifted Italy to third place in the team event. The brothers also collected team bronze medals in the 1964 Games in Tokyo and again in the 1976 Montreal Olympics. Both were then in their fifties, and it was twenty-eight years after their Olympic debuts.

CHRISTIAN (1928) and
PIERRE (1920) D'ORIOLA
(France)

Christian and Pierre were cousins from one of the most famous sporting families in France who won Olympic fame in contrasting sports. Christian was a fencing master who specialized in the foil event. He won an individual silver in the 1948 Games and took the gold medal in 1952 and again in 1956. He also won team foil golds in 1948 and 1952 and a silver in 1956. Noted for his fast reflexes, left-handed Christian dominated the world championships in the foil for more than ten years. Pierre, the son of a leading French horseman, was a genius of a show-jumper with a temperament suited to the big occasion. He won the individual gold medal in the 1952 Olympics and regained the title in Tokyo twelve years later in the closing competition to win France's only gold medal of the Games. In 1968 he helped France win their second successive team silver and he was world champion in 1966.

JOHNNY DOUGLAS
Great Britain (1882-1930)

For sheer sporting versatility, Johnny Douglas took some beating. He was Olympic middleweight boxing champion in London in 1908, outpointing Australian Snowy Baker in what was considered a classic contest. He also played amateur football for England and the Corinthians and captained England's cricket team in fifteen of his twenty-three Test appearances.

His initials were JWT and he was known throughout the cricket world as 'Johnny Won't Hit Today' Douglas because of his stubborn, defensive batting displays against Australia. He captained Essex for fourteen seasons from 1911 and was famed and feared for his tough discipline and his competitive attitude. He scored nearly 25,000 runs during his career, and took 1894 wickets, including the dismissal of five Yorkshire batsmen in eight balls at Leyton in 1905. Douglas was tragically drowned at the age of forty-eight while trying to rescue his father following a boating accident off the coast of Denmark in December 1930.

GUY DRUT
France (1950)

A silver medallist in the 1972 Olympic 110 metres hurdles final, Guy Drut predicted that he would win the gold medal in the 1976 Games in 13.28 sec. He then put action where his mouth was and achieved exactly what he had forecast, resisting a late challenge from Cuban Alejandro Casanas to win in 13.28 sec (which was later rounded up to 13.3 sec). An adviser on sport to the French Prime Minister, Drut was often booed by French spectators who disagreed with his political views, but they were all cheering him when he became the first Frenchman to win an Olympic track title since Joseph Guillemot's victory in the 5000 metres in Antwerp in 1920. Drut, who has an English mother, was born in the same street in the small town of Oignies as former French track hero Michel Jazy, an Olympic silver medallist in the 1500 metres in Rome.

EDDIE EAGAN
United States (1898)

Eddie Eagan is a unique Olympic hero. He was a member of the United States team that won the four-man bobsleigh title at the 1932 Olympics, which made him the first competitor to win gold medals at both the winter and summer celebrations of the Games. Twelve years earlier he had won an Olympic boxing championship by beating Norwegian Sverre Sorsdal in the light-heavyweight final in the 1920 Antwerp Games. Eagan, who studied at Yale and then Oxford, later became head of the New York Boxing Commission and an authoritative figure in world professional boxing.

HERB ELLIOTT
Australia (1938)

Herb Elliott was perfection on two legs. He retired from athletics at the age of twenty-two as the unquestioned Master of the Mile and as an Olympic champion whose running display in the 1500 metres final in the 1960 Rome Games was simply awe-inspiring. Urged on by his coach and mentor Percy

Herb Elliott: perfection on two legs

Cerutty, he took the lead 600 metres from the finish and shattered his rivals with a sustained sprint that carried him to victory by a margin of 20 metres and in a world record 3 min 35.6 sec. It was one of the greatest track performances in Olympic history.

Born at Subiaco near Perth, Elliott was an outstanding junior athlete and set a string of under-nineteen world bests before proving himself a formidable force in the senior ranks. He ran his first sub four minute mile in 1958 at the age of nineteen and during a European tour later in the same year chopped the world mile record to 3 min 55.4 sec and the 1500 metres record to 3 min 36 sec. Trained unmercifully hard by the fanatical and dedicated Cerutty, Elliott won the 880 yards and mile titles in the 1958 Commonwealth Games. He broke the four-minute mile barrier seventeen times during his short but sensational career and was never once beaten over the mile or metric mile distance. At his peak, he attracted a $200,000 offer to turn professional but he preferred to run for fun and when the pressures of fame punctured the enjoyment of it all he retired with plenty of running still left in him.

PAUL ELVSTROM
Denmark (1928)
Paul Elvstrom is among the greatest small-boat racing sailors of all time. He was just nineteen when he won the first of four Olympic gold medals in the 1948 London Games in the Firefly class. At the next three Olympics he sailed to championship victories in the Finn class. He believed in being physically as well as mentally fit for racing and used to follow a daily programme of exercises while sitting on a boat simulator. It was an approach that paid handsome dividends. He won eleven world championships in seven different classes between 1957 and 1974 and made the most of his success by starting a boat-designing business. It caused controversy about his amateur status but did nothing to dent his standing as a legendary man of the sea. Temper overruled his talent in the 1972 Munich Games when he was bidding for a fifth successive gold medal. He just couldn't get his act together in the Soling class and in a fit of anger and frustration quit midway through the competition.

KORNELIA ENDER
East Germany (1959)
A silver medallist at the age of thirteen in the Munich Olympics, Kornelia Ender had blossomed into the greatest all-round woman swimmer in the world by the time of the Montreal Games four years later. She proved her superiority by winning four gold medals, a record haul in women's Olympic swimming. No country in the world can approach East Germany's thoroughness for sports training and organization and Kornelia was the product of a carefully program-

Kornelia Ender: the mermaid of the Montreal Games

med training schedule that brought sneers from some of her outdistanced rivals that she was like a robot in the water. 'I have had the advantage of scientific preparation,' she conceded. 'But the talent has to be there in the first place.' Few could argue with that point of view.

Kornelia had first started swimming in her hometown of Plauen, encouraged by her parents who were worried that she was developing a walking defect. Her potential was spotted during a schools swimming gala and she was given specialized coaching from the age of ten. In the world championships of 1973 and 1975 and also in the European championships of 1974 she amassed a total of twelve gold medals. This was all just a prelude to her golden splash in the 1976 Olympics by which time weight training had shaped her once sylph-like 5ft 10in figure into a powerful eleven-stone frame. Kornelia spurted to world records and victories in the 100 and 200 metres freestyle and the 100 metres butterfly and helped East Germany to a gold medal and a silver in the relays. Her fiancé Roland Matthes, a double gold medallist in the backstroke events in the Olympics of 1968 and 1972, cheered her on from the poolside and added a backstroke bronze medal to his own unique collection.

LEE EVANS
United States (1947)

From the age of nineteen when he won the 1966 US 400 metres championship to a remarkable Olympic victory in Mexico in 1968, Lee Evans was the undisputed king of one-lap racing. He won every major championship he entered, including the Pan American Games 400 metres crown in 1967 and three more US titles. His most memorable triumph came in the thin air of Mexico in 1968 when he powered to the gold medal in a mind-blowing 43.86 sec, a record that survives 16 years later. On the morning of his great victory Evans had been on the point of pulling out of the race because of a decision to expel his Black team-mates Tommie Smith and John Carlos following a human rights demonstration with which he was sympathetic. Smith and Carlos persuaded him to go ahead and run...and that he certainly did! Californian Evans had only one major flop during his career when he finished fourth in the 1972 Olympic trials just a few weeks after beating Vince Matthews, his eventual successor as Olympic gold medallist, in the US Championships. He turned professional later in the year but applied for reinstatement as an amateur and proved he was still a world-class athlete in 1980 when he ran a 46.5 sec 400 metres. Evans shared in three relay world records and set a world's 600 metres record of 1 min 14.3 sec.

RAY EWRY
United States (1873-1937)

Ray Ewry: developed explosive power

Doctors told Ray Ewry's parents soon after his birth that he would never be able to walk, since he had been paralysed by polio. He was confined to a wheelchair until another doctor devised for him a series of exercises aimed at getting strength into his legs. He developed explosive power and became the king of the standing jumps, then popular athletic events. Ewry jumped to ten Olympic gold medals, including two in the 1906 'Interim' Games. He won fifteen US national titles and his world standing long-jump record of 11ft 4⅞in survived until 1938 when the event was finally discarded. Ewry, born in Lafayette, Indiana, was Olympic champion in the standing high jump, long jump and triple jump in 1900 and 1904 and — after the triple jump had been deleted from the programme — retained the high-jump and long-jump gold medals in London in 1908. A gangling 6ft 3 in tall and weighing just over 10 stone, Ewry was twenty-seven before he made his Olympic debut in Paris. His main motivation came from a wife who was as ambitious for success as he was himself, and she used to cheer — some say nag — him on from the side of the jumping pits.

CHRIS FINNEGAN
Great Britain (1944)
Cheerful Chris Finnegan collected Britain's first boxing gold medal for twelve years when he won the middleweight title in the 1968 Games in Mexico, but it was the early hours of the morning and five hours after his triumph before his victory became official. That was how long it took Chris to produce the necessary urine sample to prove he had not taken any illegal stimulant. An Olympic medical adviser, equipped with an empty bottle, had to accompany him to his victory party in a Mexican restaurant and it took eight pints of beer before Chris could provide the long-awaited evidence at precisely 1.40 a.m!

Finnegan, born in Buckinghamshire but a chirpy Cockney in his personality and accent, was a stylish southpaw who relied more on boxing skills than punching power to outmanoeuvre opponents. He outpointed three fellow southpaws on the way to the final and then jabbed his way to a narrow points victory over Russian favourite Alexei Kiseliov. He turned professional two months after his Olympic triumph and became British, European and Commonwealth light-heavyweight champion before a gallant bid for the world title against American Bob Foster ended with a fourteenth-round knockout defeat. Chris was forced to retire following an eye operation in 1975 but his younger brother, Kevin, carried on the Finnegan fighting tradition and captured the British and European middleweight titles.

EDWIN FLACK
Australia (1874-?)
Edwin (Teddy) Flack was the forerunner of the great flock of formidable middle-distance runners from Down Under. He was Australia's first ever mile champion (clocking 4 min 44 sec) in 1893. Two years later he came to England to study accountancy and also to gain international running experience. He took a month's holiday from his clerical job to join the small band of British athletes bound for Athens in 1896 for the revival of the Olympics. On the first day he qualified for the 800 metres final and on the second day won the 1500 metres title in 4 min 33.2sec.

He was Australia's only competitor in the Games and the organizers were so confused that as he was being presented with the victor's laurel wreath they raised the Austrian flag and then the Union Jack, which led to him being listed in some record books as representing Great Britain. Pacing himself carefully through two identical laps of 65.5 seconds, Flack won the 800 metres and then, rather than rest on his laurels, tried to make it a hat-trick of victories in the marathon. Before the race he was introduced to the British Ambassador who was so impressed by his attitude that he 'loaned' him his butler to cycle around the course with him. Both Flack and the butler, resplendent in bowler hat and black suit, were choked by dust being kicked up by the accompanying Greek cavalry and had to abandon the race while contesting the lead with eventual winner Spiridon Louis.

JOHN J. FLANAGAN
United States (1868-1938)
John J. Flanagan was the first of the great 'Irish Invincibles' who dominated the hammer-throwing event in the first quarter of this century. The mighty man from Limerick is recognized as the 'Father' of hammer-throwing. During what was literally a long throwing career that spanned twenty years, he increased the world record sixteen times and became the first athlete to win three successive Olympic titles. He was an all-rounder as a teenager in Ireland, winning local championships as a sprinter and long-jumper as well as in all the throwing events.

Flanagan emigrated to the United States when he was twenty-three and started to specialize in the hammer event after joining the New York police force. He won the first of seven American championships in 1897 and was Olympic champion in Paris in 1900 and again in St Louis in 1904. A veteran of forty by the time of the London Olympics in 1908, he produced an Olympic record throw of 170ft 4¼in to complete a hat-trick of gold medals. The two runners-up, Matt McGrath and bronze medallist Con Walsh, were also born in Ireland. McGrath, who had taken over from Flanagan as world record holder, was wearing a United States vest and Walsh was representing Canada. Flanagan, who inspired a generation of Irish athletes to concentrate on the throwing events, also won a silver medal in the 56 lb weight in the 1904 Olympics and finished fourth in the discus. He died in his native Ireland in 1938 at the age of seventy.

GEORGE FOREMAN
United States (1948)

The awesome power and stunning potential of George Foreman was displayed for all to see in the heavyweight final in the 1968 Mexico Olympics. His clubbing blows destroyed the defence of Ionas Chepulis and the referee intervened in the second round to save the outgunned Russian from unnecessary punishment. It was difficult to believe that this was only Foreman's twenty-first amateur contest. His crushing victory was the first of many sensations in his career.

Foreman, a former social worker born in a Black ghetto in Marshall, Texas, turned professional six months after his Olympic triumph and won his first thirty-seven fights in impressive style. But he was still a betting underdog when he climbed into the ring in Kingston, Jamaica, in January, 1973, to challenge Joe Frazier — the 1964 Olympic champion — for sport's richest prize, the world heavyweight title. Foreman suddenly took on a mantle of invincibility as he demolished Frazier, knocking him to the canvas six times before the referee rescued the beaten favourite in the second round. The new champion then ended Ken Norton's challenge in two one-sided rounds before putting his title and unbeaten record on the line against Muhammad Ali in Zaïre in October 1974. Ali produced one of the greatest performances of his headline-hitting career, knocking out a baffled and exhausted Foreman in round eight after soaking up all the dethroned champion's best punches.

Foreman was never the same fighter after that defeat by Ali and suddenly turned his back on the fight game after a points loss to Jimmy Young in 1977, declaring that he had 'found God' and could no longer bring himself to punch other human beings on the nose. He decided that he would devote the rest of his life to helping social misfits, contenting himself with punching the Bible.

DICK FOSBURY
United States (1947)

Dick Fosbury revolutionized high jumping when he won the 1968 Olympic gold medal by propelling himself across the bar head first and on his back. The unorthodox and inventive technique became universally known as the 'Fosbury Flop' and has since been copied by most of the world's leading high-jumpers. He had been coached as a conventional straddle jumper at school and then switched to the old-fashioned scissors style before evolving his novel method that dramatically lifted him to new heights.

Fosbury, from Portland, Oregon, became a member of the exclusive seven-foot club in January 1968, and ten months later beat twelve straddle jumpers in

Dick Fosbury: flopped to Olympic fame

the Olympic high-jump final. The slim, 6 ft 4 in tall college student captured the imagination of the spectators in the stadium and millions of world-wide television viewers with his spectacular 'back drops'. He cleared 7ft 4¼in at his third and final attempt to edge team-mate Ed Carruthers into second place. Fosbury, who turned professional in 1973, never again quite reached the heights of his Olympic triumph, but he had written his name into athletics history as the creator of a new and extremely effective jumping style.

DAWN FRASER
Australia (1937)
This Aussie mermaid made a golden splash in the Olympic swimming pool during a career that was studded with success and sometimes scarred with controversy. At the age of fourteen she was banned from amateur competition because she had been a member of a professional swimming club, but this

harsh judgement was reversed and she became arguably the greatest woman sprint swimmer of all time. She created Olympic history by becoming the first swimmer to win a gold medal in the same event — the 100 metres freestyle — in three successive Games.

The remarkable 'Dawnie', born in Balmain, New South Wales, had her name in the world record lists thirty-nine times despite the ever-present handicap of bronchial asthma. Coached by the demanding Harry Gallagher, she was an all-rounder of enormous range and talent and won Australian titles in butterfly and individual medley events. She was an outspoken and unconventional personality who often crossed swords with officialdom. Her third Olympic title came in Tokyo in 1964 in an Olympic record 59.5 sec just a matter of months after she had survived a car smash in which her mother was killed. There was a controversial climax to her eventful career when she was banned from the sport she had graced with her talent. She admitted being one of the perpetrators of a prank that involved the removal of the official flag from the Emperor's Palace in Tokyo. Her devastating ten-year suspension was lifted after four years but by

Dawn Fraser: the golden girl of the pool

then Dawnie had given up competitive swimming. Her astonishing performances in the Olympic pool assure her of a permanent place in the swimming record books.

JOE FRAZIER
United States (1944)
Joe Frazier was earning $75 a week as a slaughter-house worker in Philadelphia when he won the Olympic heavyweight title in 1964. Seven years later he shared a $5 million purse with Muhammad Ali in a world heavyweight championship contest in New York that lived up to its billing as 'The Fight of the Century.' Frazier knocked Ali down in the fifteenth and final round to clinch a points victory and to stretch his unbeaten record as a professional to twenty-seven bouts. Two fights later Frazier's world fell apart when he was hammered to a two-round defeat in a title defence against George Foreman, the man who succeeded him as Olympic heavyweight champion.

'Billy Joe' Frazier was the seventh son in a family of thirteen and was raised on a South Carolina vegetable plantation in circumstances close to the poverty line. He married at sixteen and moved to Philadelphia to find work. It was because of an increasing weight problem that he took to boxing. Trainer Yank Durham saw him working out in the gymnasium run by the Police Athletic Club and persuaded him to box as an amateur. Frazier was beaten by Buster Mathis in the US Olympic trials but was sent to Tokyo after his conqueror had broken a thumb. He knocked out two opponents in the first round, then ko'd Russian champion Vadim Yemelyanov in the second round of their semi-final and clinched the gold medal by outpointing West German Hans Huber.

Frazier, 5ft 11½in tall and a solid fifteen stone, had a perpetual-motion style of fighting that earned him the nickname the 'Black Marciano.' He was more popularly known as 'Smokin' Joe' because of the way he would switch from being a quiet, friendly charac-ter to a fiery, aggressive warrior the moment the first bell rang. Joe retired in 1976 after two defeats by Ali and a failure to get revenge over Foreman. They were the only two men to beat him in a 36-fight professio-nal career. He continues to be closely associated with boxing as manager and trainer of two fighting sons, one of whom — Marvis — challenged Larry Holmes for Joe's old world heavyweight crown in 1983.

GERT FREDRIKSSON
Sweden (1919)
There was good reason for Swedish kayak master Gert Fredriksson to be known as the 'King of the Waterways.' He was almost unbeatable throughout a 25-year career that started when he was seventeen. His honours haul included six Olympic gold medals, plus a silver and a bronze, seven world crowns,

twelve Nordic championships and sixty-five Swedish individual and team titles. He was twenty-eight when he won his first Olympic gold medals in the 1000 and 10,000 metres kayak events in 1948 and forty-one when he completed his collection with a shared victory in the kayak 1000 metres doubles at Rome in 1960. On the few occasions when he was beaten he always gained revenge in return duels. The mind boggles as to what his Olympic record would have been but for the intervention of the war years when he was at the peak of his powers.

RUTH FUCHS
East Germany (1946)
Ruth Fuchs monopolized women's javelin-throwing during the 1970s. She increased the world record five times, with a personal best just four centimetres short of the 'magic' 70-metres barrier. Ruth won the Olympic title in Munich in 1972 and became the first woman to retain the javelin crown in Montreal in 1976 with an Olympic record throw of 216 ft 4 in (65.94 m). She was favourite to pull off a hat-trick in Moscow in 1980 but for once in her career cracked under the pressure and had to be satisfied with eighth place. A first-rate pentathlete in her single days as Ruth Gamm, she concentrated on the javelin following marriage and continually demoralized her opponents by producing her longest distances off her first throw. She failed to win only twice in the twelve major championships that she contested.

ROBERT GARRETT
United States (1875-?)
Princeton University student Robert Garrett had never seen a discus before he arrived in Athens for the revival of the Olympics in 1896. It was the one competition the Greeks were convinced they would win. In fact tradition demanded it, and the famous classical Myron statue, the Discus Thrower, was studied for hints on the technique of the ancient Greeks who had created the event. Garrett had practised with what he *thought* was a discus at Princeton, but the makeshift implement was twelve inches in diameter and weighed twenty pounds. He took a couple of throws with it and then decided that discus-throwing was all Greek to him. When he saw the Greeks training for the discus he was pleasantly surprised to find it much smaller and lighter than the one he had been heaving about at Princeton. He entered at the last minute just to warm up for his speciality event, the shot-put, and startled himself and shattered the Greeks by winning with a final throw of 95 ft 7¾ in (29.15 m). Garrett, a wealthy young man who paid for three of his Princeton colleagues to make the trip to compete in Athens, went on to win the shot, and he also finished second in the long jump and third in the high jump.

ANTON GEESINK
Holland (1934)

This man-mountain — 6ft 6in tall and weighing around twenty stone — went to Japan, the home of judo, and won the prized gold medal in the Open competition at the 1964 Olympics. He was a dominant force in the judo world from the time when he won his first world title in 1961 until his retirement in 1967. Considering his bulk, he was remarkably quick and agile and used to beat opponents with a combination of skill, speed and strength. He collected the first of eighteen European titles in 1952 at the age of eighteen and became totally dedicated to improving his fitness and technique. The result of all his hard work was that he became the first man to conquer the Japanese at the sport they had created. He retired at thirty-three to concentrate on coaching young judo experts who had been inspired by his world-beating exploits.

VLADIMIR GOLUBNICHI
USSR (1936)

His long walking career made him a legendary figure in his sport. Born in the Ukraine district of Sumy, he was a world-class walker for a period of eighteen years, during which he never finished outside the first three in seven Olympic and European 20-kilometre championship races. He set his first world record at the age of nineteen and won the Olympic gold medals for his speciality event in 1960 and 1968. Golubnichi, a school-teacher, took the bronze in the 1964 Olympic 20-kilometre walk won by Britain's Ken Matthews and was the silver medallist in 1972, just seventy metres behind East German Peter Frenkel. He won the European title in 1974 after a third and a second in his previous bids for the championship, and two years later — at the age of forty — finished seventh in the Montreal Olympics with a lifetime's best clocking of 83 min 55 sec.

DUNCAN GOODHEW
Great Britain (1957)

Duncan Goodhew's bald head made him as easily recognizable as Kojak to television audiences during the 1980 Olympics. A member of the Beckenham Swimming Club, the former Millfield schoolboy took full advantage of the absence of the crack Americans to win the 100 metres breaststroke gold medal in 1 min 3.34 sec. He was also sixth in the 200 metres breaststroke final and helped Britain pick up a bronze in the 4 x 100 metres medley relay. Duncan's inspiring influence on the British team stretched beyond the pool and his bubbling personality made him one of the most popular figures in the 1980

Duncan Goodhew: an inspiring influence

Games. He had swum in the shadow of David Wilkie in the 1976 Montreal Olympics, when he finished seventh in the 100 metres breaststroke final. He left his Yapton, Sussex, home for a scholarship in the United States where he improved his technique and toughened his competitive attitude. Sharpened by coach Dave Haller, he had hoped to beat the 100 metres breaststroke world record in Moscow but later admitted he had become too excited and worked up before the final, wasting too much essential adrenalin.

SHANE GOULD
Australia (1956)

Few people have ever worked so hard for golden glory as Shane Gould, a freckle-faced, fifteen-year-old schoolgirl who dominated the women's swimming in the 1972 Olympics in Munich. In the four-month build-up to the Games Shane had been getting up every morning at 4.30 a.m. to train for speed and stamina and she had covered nearly a thousand miles in the swimming pool in her final preparations for a punishing schedule of fifteen races in eight days. In the previous year, she had revealed her astonishing ability by breaking every freestyle world record from 100 to 1500 metres.

Shane Gould: won the war of nerves

Shane, born in Brisbane during the 1956 Melbourne Olympics and the great-great-granddaughter of a man called Fish, was a quiet, unassuming girl but claims were being made on her behalf that she would win a record five gold medals in Munich. Her American rivals countered by launching a psychological war of nerves against her, going to and from the Olympic pool in sweaters emblazoned with the message 'All that glitters is not Gould.' But despite all the enormous pressure on her, she managed to pick up glittering prizes by winning the 200 and 400 metres freestyle titles and the 200 metres individual medley and she set a world record in each event. She also won a silver in the 800 metres freestyle and a bronze in the 100 metres freestyle behind American supergirls Sandy Neilson and Shirley Babashoff.

JUDY GRINHAM
Great Britain (1939)

When Judy Grinham won the 100 metres backstroke title in the European championships in Budapest in 1958 she became the first swimmer ever to hold Olympic, Commonwealth and European titles at the same time. Her greatest moment had come two years earlier in the 1956 Melbourne Games when she had come from behind to win the 100 metres backstroke gold medal in an Olympic record 1 min 12.9 sec. It made her Britain's first swimming gold medallist for thirty-two years. Judy, whose Hampstead club had

accepted her membership application only at the third time of asking, competed at top level for barely two years before her triumph in Melbourne. She was so badly affected by pre-race nerves in the final that she was trailing in fifth place at the halfway point, but she launched a tremendous sprint finish that carried her to victory by just a fingertip from American favourite Carin Cone. She established herself as one of Britain's greatest ever swimmers over the next two years and by the time of her retirement in 1959 at the age of twenty she had won four major championships and had set three individual and shared in two relay world records.

ARCHIE HAHN
United States (1880-?)
Archie Hahn — 'The Milwaukee Meteor' — won a unique set of gold medals in the 1904 Olympics in St Louis. These were the only Games that included a 60 metres dash along with the traditional 100 and 200 metres and he won all three events. His victory over a straight course in the 200 metres was unusual in that he was given a metre start over his three rivals in the final. They were all ordered to begin a metre back behind the line after three false starts which it was alleged Hahn himself had caused by rocking on the line in a pretence at setting off. He won in 21.6 sec, which survived as an Olympic record for twenty-eight years. Hahn, born in Dodgeville, Wisconsin, went to Athens for the 'Interim Olympics' in 1906 and won the 100 metres in 11.2 sec — a fifth of a second slower than his winning time in St Louis.

OLIVER HALASSY
Hungary (1905)
No list of Olympic heroes would be complete without the inclusion of Oliver Halassy, one of the greatest water-polo players of all time. He was a key member of the Hungarian team that won a silver medal in Amsterdam in 1928 and then collected successive gold medals in the Olympics of 1932 and 1936. What set Halassy apart from other Olympic competitors was that he had only one leg. He was knocked down by a tram in his native Budapest when an eleven-year-old schoolboy and had to have a leg amputated. Despite his handicap, he was capped ninety-six times by Hungary as a master of water-polo and was once also European 1500 metres freestyle champion. A true hero.

MURRAY HALBERG
New Zealand (1933)
Olympic champions have rarely come braver or more determined than Murray Halberg, whose promising rugby-playing career was ended in 1950 by a match accident that left him with a paralysed shoulder and a withered left arm. He switched to athletics and gradually over the next twelve years established himself as one of the boldest runners ever to set foot on the track. The most memorable moment of his career came in the Olympic 5000 metres final in Rome in 1960 when he gambled everything on a break for home with three laps still to go. He left his rivals floundering with a 'suicidal' 61 sec lap and then kept himself going by sheer willpower over the last 800 metres in scorching-hot conditions that made every step a challenge. His spurt had opened a lead of twenty metres and this had been cut to just eight metres by the chasing pack as Halberg, close to exhaustion, crossed the finishing line in 13 min 43.4 sec.

Halberg was coached by the knowledgeable Arthur Lydiard, who was the man behind that other gifted New Zealand track hero of the 1960s, Peter Snell. During a tour of Europe in 1961, Halberg set new world records for two and three miles and shared in a 4 x one mile relay world record. He had started his athletics career as a miler, finishing fifth in the historic 'Mile of the Century' when Roger Bannister beat John Landy in the 1954 Empire Games in Edmonton. Two years later, he came one from last in the Olympic 1500 metres final in Melbourne and decided he would be best off concentrating on longer distances. He wound down his eventful career by retaining his Commonwealth Games three miles title at Perth in 1962, outsprinting Ron Clarke from the bell for a last lap of 53.8 sec and victory in 13 min 48.8 sec. It was a win that underlined his tactical brilliance because everybody in the field had been waiting for him to make his characteristic break with two or more laps to go, as in Rome two years earlier. But Halberg outfoxed and outgunned them all.

LARS HALL
Sweden (1927)
Baron Pierre de Coubertin, the French aristocrat who revived the Olympics in 1896, suggested the inclusion of the modern pentathlon in the Olympic programme because he considered it the supreme test of the sporting all-rounder. Lars Hall, born in Karlskrona in 1927, proved himself a supreme champion by becoming the first man to win successive gold medals in the punishing event in which competitors are tested at shooting, swimming, fencing, horse riding and finally with a run against the clock over a gruelling cross-country course. Hall was Olympic champion in 1952 and 1956, which followed his world championship victories of 1950 and 1951. He was the first non-military winner of the Olympic title.

WYNDHAM HALSWELLE
Great Britain (1883-1916)
There has never been a lonelier Olympic champion than Wyndham Halswelle, a proud Scot who was a

lieutenant in the British Army at the time of his gold medal victory in the 1908 Games at London's White City. He was a central figure in one of the most controversial incidents in Olympic history which climaxed with him running the 400 metres final on his own. He originally had three American rivals — J.C.Carpenter, W.C.Robbins and J.P.Taylor, who was bidding to become the first black Olympic champion. There were no lanes to discipline the runners on the horseshoe-shaped third of a mile White City track and in a free-for-all finish coming into the home straight Carpenter appeared to make Halswelle chop his stride by taking a diagonal path to the finishing line. A straw-hatted British official stepped on to the track and snapped the tape before Carpenter could break it in first place.

It was decided to disqualify Carpenter after a detective-style study of the footprints on the cinder track. The Americans, already fuming over earlier chauvinistic judgments by the British officials, considered a mass withdrawal from the Games and Robbins and Taylor withdrew in protest from the planned re-run of the race. This left Halswelle on his own, and with great dignity he made a circuit of the track in 50 seconds for the only walkover victory in Olympic history. He had set an Olympic record of 48.4 sec in the semi-finals and had proved his outstanding ability two years earlier when winning the 100, 220, 440 and 880 yards titles in the space of one afternoon in the Scottish championships. The United States team dropped their walkout threat, and J.P.Taylor achieved his ambition of becoming the first black Olympic champion when he shared in the medley relay victory. Sadly, there was tragedy around the corner for both Halswelle and Taylor. The Scot was killed in action during the First World War, and Taylor died of typhoid just a matter of months after his triumph in London.

TOMMY HAMPSON
Great Britain (1907-1965)
Tommy Hampson struggled in last in the half-mile event in the 1929 Oxford v. Cambridge match, and onlookers must have wondered why he bothered to torture himself on the track for so little reward. Just three years later he was crowned the two-lap Olympic champion. The bespectacled Londoner won the 800 metres final in the 1932 Los Angeles Olympics in a world record 1 min 49.7 sec. His winning time meant he was the first man to break the 1 min 50 sec barrier, and also that he had improved an astonishing ten seconds in the three years since his laboured run for Oxford in the varsity match. Hampson, the son of a good-class middle-distance runner, developed a marvellous judgment of pace, as he proved in the Olympic final. He knew exactly the time of which he was capable and set out to run two identical laps, regardless of the pace set by any of his rivals. He ran the first lap in 54.8 sec and was fifteen metres down

on race leader Phil Edwards at the bell. Hampson unleashed a winning surge off the last bend and completed the second lap in 54.7 sec for a beautifully judged victory.

FRED HANSEN
United States (1940)
Texas dentist Fred Hansen must have felt like one of the patients waiting to face his drill as he prepared to make a final attempt at the pole-vault height of 16 ft 8¾ in in the 1964 Tokyo Olympics. The world record holder at 17 ft 4 in, Hansen had been locked in a nine-hour-long battle with three Germans and the odds were suddenly on victory going to Wolfgang Reinhardt, who had cleared at 16ft 6¾in after Hansen had elected to pass at that height. What added to the pressure on Hansen was the knowledge that the United States had won every pole-vault competition since the revival of the Olympics in 1896. He was defending a nation's pride and tradition as he started his run watched by a hushed crowd who had stayed late into the night to witness an absorbing contest. Hansen soared like a bird into the floodlit sky and made a magnificent clearance. Then it was Reinhardt's turn for a nerve-testing make or break vault. He dislodged the bar and so Hansen was the Olympic champion, the first to win the title using a fibre-glass pole.

At the age of eighteen, Hansen set a Texas high-school record of 13ft 7in with a steel pole but it was not until he switched to fibre-glass three years later that he suddenly emerged as a world-class vaulter. He twice raised the world record in 1964 before his victory in Tokyo, after which he decided to retire while (quite literally) at the top.

GLENN HARDIN
United States (1910)
Glenn Hardin's first 400 metres hurdles world record was set in odd circumstances. He finished second behind Ireland's Bob Tisdall in the Olympics final in Los Angeles in 1932, yet had the consolation of being credited with a world record of 52.00 sec. Tisdall ran 0.3 sec faster but knocked down the tenth and last hurdle, which in those days ruled out record recognition. Two years later Hardin twice lowered the world record while leading the way through the tape. He clocked 51.8 sec at a meeting in Milwaukee, Wisconsin, in June 1934, and a month later chopped a whopping 1.2 sec off the record when winning an invitation race in Stockholm. His remarkable time of 50.6 sec survived as a world record for nearly twenty years.

Hardin was one of the world's leading flat one-lap

Opposite
Bob Hayes: the fastest thing on two legs

runners and clocked a personal best 46.8 sec in 1934, his peak year in which he also set an unofficial world record of 22.7 sec for 220 yards hurdles over a straight course. He had been the favourite for the gold medal in the 440 yards hurdles in Los Angeles but made no mistake four years later in Berlin, winning in 52.4 sec. Hardin's retirement a few weeks later was clouded in controversy when he lent his name to a nationwide advertising campaign in which he stated that he smoked both during and after his meals. One of his rivals commented: 'The only time I saw Glenn smoking was when he disappeared ahead of me in a puff of smoke!'

BOB HAYES
United States (1942)
Bob Hayes produced a succession of phenomenal performances during his brief athletics career to guarantee himself considerable support in the argument as to who has been the greatest sprinter of the century. Hayes did not start taking an interest in athletics until he was sixteen, but quickly revealed his potential with an unofficial 9.3 sec 100 yards which equalled the then world record. Over the next five years he became the first man to run 100 yards in 9.1 sec, the first to break six seconds for the indoor 60 yards dash and one of the few men to duck under 10.00 seconds for 100 metres.

His sub-10 run came in the semi-final of the Olympic 100 metres in Tokyo in 1964, but his 9.9 sec was not recognized as a world record because of a following wind. In the final the 'Black Bullet' left a top-class field for dead as he sped to victory in a legitimate world record equalling 10.00 sec — with hand timing (subsidiary to the electronic timing) stopping at 9.9 sec, a remarkable run on a cinder track and at sea level. He was several times clocked exceeding 27 miles per hour and his last-leg sprint relay runs lifted him into the land of legend. In one baton charge he was timed at 7.8 sec for 100 yards, and when anchorman for the United States team in the 4 x 100 metres relay final in 1964 he set off three metres behind the leaders and led by the same margin as he stopped the clock in a world record 39.00 sec. Hayes also equalled the world record for 220 yards and 200 metres but the shorter events were his speciality. His pigeon-toed, rolling action meant he was not the prettiest sight on earth but he was certainly the fastest thing on two legs, and the immense power he put into his running served him well when he became a successful professional footballer with Dallas Cowboys soon after his Olympic triumph.

DAVID HEMERY
Great Britain (1944)
David Hemery was one of Britain's most emphatic and impressive Olympic champions. He won the 400

metres hurdles final in Mexico in 1968 by the astonishing margin of seven metres and in a world record 48.12 sec. He completed a full set of Olympic medals in Munich four years later, when he took a bronze medal in a gallant defence of his title and a silver in the 4 x 400 metres relay. Hemery was a fine advertisement for both British and American athletics. Born in Cirencester, Gloucestershire, he moved with his family to the United States when he was twelve and six years later returned to Britain, where he started to establish himself as a hurdler of great promise. He won the AAA junior 120 yards title — an event in which he was Commonwealth champion in 1966 — and in his debut over 440 yards hurdles finished third in the 1962 Midlands championships in 58.6 sec.

Returning to the United States in 1964, he began to make startling progress while studying at Boston University. He was coached in England by veteran Fred Housden, a champion pole-vaulter in the 1920s, and in America by the knowledgable Bill Smith. Hemery went to Mexico as fourth favourite behind the three American challengers, who had all recorded faster times than had the slim, 6ft 1½ in fair-haired Briton. Yet Hemery ran like a man possessed in the final, leading from gun to finishing-line with a determination and aggression never before seen in the event. He knocked an unbelievable seven-tenths of a second off the previous world record in what was one of the greatest track performances in Olympic history. Hemery later became a good-class decathlete and set a UK record of 13.6 sec for 110 metres hurdles but it was for his astounding victory in Mexico City that he will always be remembered.

JON HENRICKS
Australia (1935)
Australia ruled the waves when Jon Henricks was at his peak and he led his country's blitz on the swimming gold medals at the 1956 Melbourne Olympics. He won the 100 metres freestyle title in 55.4 sec, which was later accepted as a world record when it was decided that short-course pool records should be erased. He had a memorable battle in the final with fellow-Aussies John Devitt and Gary Chapman, and touched home first by 0.4 sec to lead a clean sweep of the medals. Four days later he anchored the Australian 4 x 200 metres relay team to another gold-medal success. Henricks, a triple gold medallist in the Empire Games in Vancouver in 1954, would doubtless have made an even bigger impression in the Olympic swimming pool but for an ear infection knocking him out of the 1952 Games and a stomach complaint wrecking his chances of retaining his title in Rome. He originally trained as a long-distance swimmer when at school in Sydney and developed

Opposite
David Hemery (402): a full set of Olympic medals

stamina to go with his speed. He was offered a scholarship at Harvard University in 1953 but preferred to stay in home waters, where his performances made him a national idol.

ALBERT HILL
Great Britain (1889-1969)
The First World War seemed to have destroyed Albert Hill's ambitions of winning an Olympic title. He served in the British Army throughout the war when at the peak of his running powers. By the time of the first post-war Olympics in Antwerp in 1920 railwayman Hill was thirty-one years old and approaching the end of the line ten years after winning his first major honour, the AAA four miles title. He was faced with a punishing schedule of seven races in eight days as he chased an ambitious treble in the 800 and 1500 metres and the 3000 metres team race. Snatching sleep at every opportunity between races, Hill won the 800 metres final in a British record 1 min 53.4 sec, and then he captured the 1500 metres gold medal after a thrilling final straight duel with British team-mate Philip Noel-Baker (who later became more famous as a Nobel Peace Prize winner). To round it all off, Hill — the eight-day wonder — collected a silver medal in the 3000 metres team race.

Born in Tooting, Surrey, Hill was coached by Sam Mussabini who had advised top sprinters Harold Abrahams and Willie Applegarth. He produced perhaps the greatest performance of his career a year after his Olympic exploits when he chopped three seconds off the nineteen-year-old British mile record to win the AAA title at Stamford Bridge in 4 min 13.8 sec. Hill then turned professional before becoming a distinguished coach whose pupils included Sydney Wooderson, the British track hero who brought the world mile record down to 4 min 6.4 sec in 1937.

JIM HINES
United States (1946)
Jim Hines can be bracketed with Bob Hayes as arguably the fastest man of the century. He won the 100 metres gold medal in the thin air of Mexico City in 1968 in 9.95 sec — equalling the world record he had set in the US championships at Sacramento four months earlier. Coached by 1956 triple gold medallist sprinter Bobby Joe Morrow, Hines was a relay specialist in the Hayes mould. He ran a magnificent anchor leg to take the United States to victory and a world record of 38.2 sec in Mexico after collecting the baton two metres down on Cuban Enrique Figuerola and beating him to the tape by a full metre.

Hines, 6ft tall and a muscular 12 st 13 lb, was a married student at Texas Southern University at the time of his splendid running in Mexico. He had been a schoolboy prodigy, clocking a wind-assisted 9.6 sec 100 yards at the age of fifteen. Two years later he clocked a legitimate 9.4 sec to equal the American high-school record set by his idol Jesse Owens in 1933. Like Bob Hayes, he cashed in on his fame by signing as a professional with an American football team. Unlike Hayes, he struggled to adjust to his new sport and collected the unflattering nickname of 'No Hands Hines'. He also raced as a professional, once against a racehorse when he clocked 20.2 sec over 220 yards.

CLARENCE HOUSER
United States (1901)
Though a relatively small man, Clarence (Bud) Houser dominated the discus-throwing event during the 1920s and was the last athlete to win both the shot and the discus in the Olympics. He weighed barely thirteen stone and usually conceded three and four stone to his rivals but he proved that strength wasn't everything and evolved a technique that gave him crucial extra distance. Houser was the first discus-thrower to master the art of rotating at speed in the discus circle before the moment of release. His unique style inspired a new generation of discus-throwers and proof of its success is that he won the gold medal in the discus at the 1924 and 1928 Olympics and set a world record of 158ft 1¾in (48.20 m) in 1926. Houser, a trainee dentist, won the first of a procession of American titles at the age of twenty in 1921 as a shot-putter who was dwarfed by his opponents. By the following year the discus had become his speciality event, but he maintained his interest in the shot and at Paris in 1924 he equalled Bob Garrett's 1896 feat of winning both events.

VOLMARI ISO-HOLLO
Finland (1907-1969)
Volmari Iso-Hollo had to run in the shadow of a fleet of 'Flying Finns' but achieved enough in a long-running career to merit a place of honour among any athletic heroes. He is the only man to win two successive Olympic gold medals in the gruelling 3000 metres steeplechase, setting a record in Berlin in 1936 that survived until 1952. Iso-Hollo had some extraordinary experiences in the Los Angeles Olympics of 1932. On the first day he collected a silver medal in a punishing 10,000 metres race. The next day he set an Olympic record of 9 min 14.6 sec in a heat of the 3000 metres steeplechase. He then had to work overtime before winning the steeplechase final. One of the lap judges was taken ill during the race and in the confusion Iso-Hollo and his outdistanced rivals were waved on for an extra lap. Many people considered Iso-Hollo the most naturally gifted of all the Finns and believed he could have rewritten the record books had he been prepared to put in as many training miles as his great predecessors Paavo Nurmi and Hannes Kolehmainen. But he preferred to take life easy off the track yet still finished with a medals

haul of two Olympic golds and a silver and bronze in the 10,000 metres. The only time he broke a world record was in a 5000 metres race in 1932 — but he had to be content with second place behind fellow Finn Lauri Lehtinen, whose name went into the record book. His 1936 Olympic record in the steeplechase of 9 min 3.8 sec was not bettered for six years, but it was 1955 before the event became recognized for world record purposes.

VYACHESLAV IVANOV
USSR (1938)

Three successive gold medals in the single sculls confirmed Vyacheslav Ivanov's reputation as the greatest Olympic sculler of all time. He was virtually unknown in 1956 when as an eighteen-year-old student he won the European single sculls. Later in the year in Melbourne he won the first of his Olympic titles, narrowly beating nineteen-year-old Australian Stuart Mackenzie with whom he was to have a series of memorable duels over the next decade. Ivanov was so overjoyed with his victory that he tossed his medal in the air in delight, and then watched in despair as it came down in the near-by stretch of water. He and his team-mates took turns diving in a search for the medal but it had gone to a watery grave. The International Olympic Committee later agreed to replace it after an appeal from the distraught Muscovite. Over the following ten years Ivanov won two world championships and three more European titles to go with his triple Olympic honours. He was a master of pace and timing, continually coming from behind with sprint finishes to beat opponents just when they thought they had the race won. ·

MARJORIE JACKSON
Australia (1931)

Marjorie Jackson's record in international athletics was just about as perfect as it could be. She won six out of six individual gold medals in the Olympic and Commonwealth Games and set world records at all four of her specialist events — 100 yards, 100 metres, 200 metres and 220 yards. She gave notice of her enormous potential when, at the age of seventeen, she twice beat the great Fanny Blankers-Koen during the 'Flying Dutchwoman's' tour of Australia a year after her four-gold blitz in the 1948 London Olympics. Known as the 'Blue Streak' because she came from the Blue Mountains mining town of Lithgow, New South Wales, Marjorie succeeded Fanny as 100 and 200 metres Olympic champion in 1952 with a devastating display of sustained sprinting. She equalled the 11.5 sec world record for 100 metres in the semi-final and final and lowered the 200 metres mark to 23.4 sec in the semi-final before winning the final by the astonishing margin of five metres.

During her swift but sweet career Marjorie beat or equalled world sprint records ten times and shared in three sprint relay world record runs as anchorwoman for the Australian quartet. She became Mrs Nelson and hung up her spikes after retaining both her 100 and 220 yard titles in the 1954 Commonwealth Games in Vancouver.

MATTI JARVINEN
Finland (1909)

'Farther still and farther' was the motto for Matti Jarvinen, who helped lay the foundations for Finland's great traditions in the javelin-throwing event. He increased the world record no fewer than ten times in a span of six years from 1930, extending to a lifetime's best of 253ft 4½in in June 1936. A month later, handicapped by a back injury, he finished fifth in the Berlin Olympics when defending the title he had won in Los Angeles in 1932. Matti was the most successful member of an amazing sporting family. His father, Werner, won the discus gold medal in the 1906 'Interim' Olympics in Athens and also competed in the 1912 and 1920 Olympics. Matti's three brothers, Yrjo, Kalle and Achilles, were all top-flight field event athletes. Achilles — so named following his father's Olympic triumph in Greece — won the silver medal in the 1928 and 1932 Olympic decathlon competition. The bespectacled Matti won eight Finnish titles and was European champion in 1934 and 1938. His first world record throw in 1930 was 234ft 9½in and he so dominated his event over the next six years that he became known around the world as Matti 'The Javelin' Jarvinen.

JOHN JARVIS
Great Britain (1872-1933)

Few British swimmers have been able to begin to match the water exploits of John (Arthur) Jarvis who during his seventeen-year career won 108 major titles. He was also one of Britain's finest water polo players and a champion of 'plunge' diving. His two Olympic successes in the Paris Games of 1900 were nothing short of remarkable. The swimming events were staged in the river Seine and he won the 1000 metres by a margin of more than 100 metres over the second man home and then beat Hungarian Zoltan Halmay in the 4000 metres by nearly eleven minutes. Halmay was one of Europe's outstanding swimmers of the period and few people could argue with the description that Jarvis put on his calling cards — 'Amateur Swimming Champion of the World'. Among his honours haul were 23 English championships at distances ranging from 440 yards to ten miles and every major European invitation event in the days when races were sponsored by Royalty: the Emperor of Austria's championship of the world...the German Kaiser's championship of Europe...Queen Victoria's Diamond Jubilee one-mile challenge race...King Edward VII Coronation Cup...the King of Italy's world championship distance race. He twice won the annual fifteen-mile swim up the river Thames against top international opposition and was noted for the powerful leg kick that earned him the nickname the 'Human Tadpole'. The idol from Leicester was the undisputed king of the British waterways but his performances are not to be found in the world record books because he retired shortly before world records were officially registered in 1908.

BRUCE JENNER
United States (1949)
Bruce Jenner made no secret of the fact that he considered himself the world's greatest all-round athlete during the build-up to the 1976 Montreal Olympics. He then fulfilled his own promises and won the decathlon with a world record score of 8618 points. Jenner was not outstanding in any one of the ten events but good at all of them; a master all-rounder. He finished third at the end of the first day of competition with this sequence of performances: 10.94 sec for the 100 metres; a 23ft 8¼ in long-jump; a 50ft 4¼in shot-put; a 6ft 8in high-jump; and at the end of the day, 47.51 sec for the 400 metres. On the second day he produced a procession of personal best performances to take the gold medal and improve his own world record by 76 points. His second-day marks were 14.84 sec in the high hurdles, 164ft 2in discus, 15ft 9in pole vault, 224ft 9in javelin, and finally a 4 min 12.61 sec in the 1500 metres, the event traditionally hated by decathletes and the only one in which he totalled less than 800 points. Back in eighteenth place at the end of the competition was a promising eighteen-year-old British decathlete called Daley Thompson, who four years later would succeed Jenner as Olympic champion and world record holder. The brash but likeable American unashamedly cashed in on his Olympic fame and is now a wealthy young man famous on coast-to-coast television in the United States as an advertising man's dream.

RAFER JOHNSON
United States (1935)
Rafer Johnson proved his fighting qualities at the age of fifteen when he trapped his left foot in a conveyor belt. It was feared his promising athletics career was over almost before it had begun, but after six weeks on crutches he returned to the track and started to sharpen the skills that were to make him the greatest all-round athlete of his time. The powerfully built black Texan made his debut in the decathlon at high school in 1953, and within eighteen months had smashed the world record. A knee injury prevented him making an all-out bid for the Olympic title in Melbourne in 1956 yet he still managed to take the silver medal behind team-mate Milton Campbell. Four years later he won the gold medal in Rome after

a stirring struggle with Formosa-born Yang Chuan-kwang, his fellow pupil at UCLA. Johnson, a world-class sprinter, hurdler and long-jumper, was beaten only twice in a dozen decathlons, raised the world record points score three times and always got the better of the other great decathlete of his era, Russian Vasiliy Kuznyetsov. He retired after the 1960 Olympics, was briefly a member of John F. Kennedy's Presidential bodyguard and started a new career in Hollywood films.

ALBERTO JUANTORENA
Cuba (1950)
'White Lightning' struck twice in the 1976 Olympic track and field finals in Montreal as Alberto Juantorena astounded the athletics world with the sheer power of his running. He was a virtual novice at 800 metre running yet devastated a top-class field to win the final in a world record 1 min 43.50 sec. The muscular, 6ft 3in Cuban then completed a unique double by winning the 400 metres in 44.26 sec, the fastest non-altitude time on record. Just a year earlier Juantorena had been recovering from two operations on his foot that interrupted his progress after he had started to establish himself as an outstanding 400 metres runner, with a personal best of 44.7 sec in 1974.

Juantorena switched to athletics from basketball at the age of nineteen and within eighteen months had broken the 46 seconds barrier. His Olympics debut in 1972 ended in the semi-finals when he was edged out of the final by just a twentieth of a second. Four years later his progress was displayed for all the world to see and admire, even though his tactics of a casual start and pulsating, long-striding finish left coaches shaking their heads in disbelief at his unconventional methods. He lowered his world 800 metres record to 1 min 43.44 sec in 1977 and repeated his 400/800 double in the World Cup. Then a long run of injuries and illness severely curtailed his training programme and he could manage 'only' fourth place in the 1980 Olympic 400 metres final. His injury jinx struck again in the 1983 world championships when he stumbled on the kerb at the end of an 800 metres race and was taken to hospital in agony. Many people thought this would end his career but Alberto is the type of character who refuses to be written off and is determined to make a challenge for an Olympic medal in Los Angeles.

DUKE KAHANAMOKU
United States (1890-1968)
For ten years, Honolulu-born Duke Kahanamoku was the world's top sprint swimmer, until he made way for his successor Johnny Weissmuller. He represented the United States in four Olympic Games and collected three gold and two silver medals. His greatest triumphs came in the 100 metres freestyle.

Alberto Juantorena: 'White Lightning' strikes twice

Duke Kahanamoku (right) with Johnny 'Tarzan' Weissmuller

He won the title in the 1912 Games and retained it in Antwerp in 1920 after the final had been re-swum following a near collision and a protest in the first race in which he also finished first in a world record 1 min 0.4 sec. Going for a hat-trick of gold medals at the age of thirty-four in the 1924 Games, he was beaten into second place by new star Johnny Weissmuller, with his brother, Sam Kahanamoku, taking the bronze medal. His performances inspired a generation of Hawaiian swimmers, including Pua and Warren Kealoha who in 1920 became the first brothers to win gold medals in the same Games. Four years later Warren was the first swimmer to retain the Olympic 100 metres backstroke title.

Duke was born in the Hawaiian palace of Princess Ruth in Honolulu but his name was not a title. He was named Duke because Queen Victoria's second son, the Duke of Edinburgh, was visiting Honolulu on the day he was born. He lowered the world 100 yards record four times and the world 100 metres record three times before his retirement after competing in the 1928 Olympics at the age of thirty-eight. Idolized in Hawaii, he became a film actor and specialized in playing the role of an island king in a series of Hollywood movies. He was appointed Sheriff of Honolulu and toured the world giving exhibitions that popularized the Hawaiian sport of surfing.

TATYANA KAZANKINA
USSR (1948)

With her small, skeletal frame, hollow cheeks and dough-white skin, Tatyana Kazankina hardly inspired confidence when she arrived in Montreal for the 1976 Olympics. However, she proved looks can be totally deceiving by emerging as the 'superwoman' of the Games, winning the 800 metres in a world record 1 min 54.94 sec and the 1500 metres in 4 min 05.5 sec which included an astonishing last-lap run of 56.9 sec. An economist from Petrovsk, Tatyana was kept busy before the 1980 Moscow Olympics with marriage and the birth of a baby daughter. She twice lowered her 1500 metres world record during the build-up to the Games and then retained her title with a superbly judged run, covering the last 800 metres in less than two minutes. Twelve days after winning her third gold medal she produced a mind-blowing run in Zurich, bringing the world 1500 metres record down to 3 min 52.5 sec — which is the equivalent of a 4 min 10 sec mile, and faster than even the peerless Paavo Nurmi ever ran in his career.

KIPCHOGE KEINO
Kenya (1940)

One of the most extraordinary and entertaining running personalities of all time, 'Kip' Keino woke a sleeping giant with his exploits over a span of ten years from the date when he made his international debut in 1962. He was Black Africa's first Olympic track champion and inspired a new wave of remarkably talented athletes from the 'Dark Continent'. Keino made a modest Olympic debut at Tokyo in 1964, finishing fifth in the 5000 metres final and just failing to qualify for the 1500 metres final. He stepped up his fitness programme while working as a police training instructor and in 1965 unleashed a sequence of amazing performances that heralded his arrival as a major power. He beat the world records for 3000 and 5000 metres and clocked 3 min 54.2 sec in the mile.

Mexico City's high altitude held no fears for Keino in the 1968 Olympics. He grew accustomed to the pace of thin-air running at a Nairobi training camp 6000 feet above sea level. His ambitious bid for treble gold in Mexico died on the first day when he dropped out of the 10,000 metres three laps from home with stomach pains. He recovered to run a 5000 metres heat and then finish second in the final. Kip saved his greatest effort for the 1500 metres, coasting through two preliminary heats and then winning the final in an Olympic record 3 min 34.9 sec — a bold, breath-taking performance that left world record

holder Jim Ryun floundering twenty metres behind in second place.

Keino made a spirited defence of his 1500 metres crown in Munich four years later, having to settle for a silver medal after being outsprinted by Finland's Pekka Vasala. He proceeded to win the 3000 metres steeplechase though a virtual novice at the event. Kip showed his tactical cunning by deliberately slowing down the pace, so that even though his rivals had better technique they could not take full advantage of his inexperience at the hurdles and water jump. A double gold medallist in the 1966 Commonwealth Games and first in the 1500 metres and third in the 5000 metres in defence of his titles in Edinburgh in 1970, Keino wound down his glorious career with a flurry of professional races in the United States before returning to Kenya to resume his career as a police inspector. He had thrilled audiences around the world with his adventurous and exciting running, and lit a torch that has been passed hand to hand by a succession of black African athletes inspired by his performances. Kip shares the same birth date — January 17 — as Muhammad Ali, and is quite properly considered 'The Greatest' at home in Kenya.

JOHN B. KELLY
United States (1890-1960)

'Jack' Kelly has a special place in Olympic history as the only man to have won two Olympic sculling gold medals on the same day. He narrowly defeated Britain's Jack Beresford in the single sculls at the 1920 Antwerp Games and then less than an hour later partnered his cousin Paul Costello to victory in the double sculls, a title they retained in 1924. Costello made it a personal hat-trick in 1928 when he paired up with Charles McIlvaine. Kelly was a bricklayer in Philadelphia and had enormous strength in his arms and upper body. He had a sequence of 126 unbeaten races leading up to the 1920 Games and as well as his solo triumphs was much in demand as an outstanding stroke for fours and eights. Kelly was refused permission to compete at Henley because his club, Vesper, had been banned for alleged infringement of the amateur code. There was some foundation to the stories that he was not welcome at Henley because he was a manual labourer.

He became an immensely wealthy man and it was of enormous satisfaction to him when his son, John B. Kelly junior, won the prestige Diamond Sculls at Henley in 1947 and again in 1949. His son competed in four Olympiads and he and his cousin Bernard Costello — Paul's son — both won medals. Kelly junior was later elected President of the Amateur Athletic Union of America and his sister Grace became a famous film star before reigning as Princess Grace of Monaco until her tragic death in a motor accident in 1982.

Opposite
Tatyana Kazankina: a 'superwoman' of the track

HANNES KOLEHMAINEN
Finland (1889-1966)

The 'Father' of all Finnish running, Hannes Kolehmainen won Olympic titles in the 1912 Games at 5000 and 10,000 metres and in the cross-country event. He had to wait eight years for his next Olympic challenge and won the marathon in 2 hr 32 min 35.8 sec. The course was later discovered to be nearly half a mile over the marathon limit and the error robbed Kolehmainen of the honour of being the first amateur to break the 2½-hour barrier. His brother, Willie, had run just inside 2 hr 30 min as a professional in 1912 and another brother, Tatu, was also one of the world's leading marathon runners of the period.

Hannes 'The Mighty' set six world records at distances ranging from 3000 to 30,000 metres, the most notable being his clocking of 14 min 36.6 sec in the 5000 metres in the Stockholm Olympics after a thrilling neck-and-neck duel with French idol Jean Bouin. Hannes won a titanic battle by a stride and it was the first time that fifteen minutes had been beaten. It lasted in the world record book until erased ten years later by Paavo Nurmi, one of a long line of 'Flying Finns' whose interest in running was stimulated by the feats of Kolehmainen. Hannes lived in the United States in the period between the 1912 and 1920 Olympics and won six USA long-distance titles.

He and 'Peerless' Paavo Nurmi had the joint honour of lighting the Olympic flame at the opening ceremony of the 1952 Olympics in Helsinki.

OLGA KORBUT
USSR (1955)

Olga Korbut captured the hearts of a world-wide television audience with a combination of her bubbling personality and her brilliant performances in the gymnasium at the 1972 Munich Olympics. She collected gold medals for the beam and floor exercises and would have finished higher than seventh overall but for a tragic slip on the asymmetric bars. The seventeen-year-old Russian, elfin-like and weighing just over six stone, lacked the majestic presence of her team-mate Ludmilla Turischeva but did more than anybody to popularize gymnastics as a compelling television sport with an adventurous style that tugged at the emotions. She added a silver medal to her collection on the beam in Montreal in 1976 when she had to bow to the superiority of Nadia Comaneci who was technically more efficient but lacking the charm and charisma that had made Olga the darling of the Games four years earlier.

Olga Korbut: the princess of the gymnasium

ALVIN KRAENZLEIN
United States (1876-1928)

One of the first great all-rounders, Alvin Kraenzlein set world records in three different events and is the only athlete to win four individual gold medals in track and field at one Olympics. He revolutionized hurdling by running rather than leaping over the barriers and created world records for 120 and 220 yards hurdles in 1898. The following year he twice increased the world long-jump record and in the 1900 Olympics in Paris won the 60 metres dash, the 110 and 200 metres hurdles and the long jump. His team-mate and bitter rival Myer Prinstein led the long-jump qualifying competition but declined to take part in the final because it was staged on a Sunday. Kraenzlein, a student at Pennsylvania University, beat Prinstein's qualifying mark by just one centimetre. He was in Germany at the outbreak of the First World War coaching the German athletics team for the 1916 Games that were cancelled.

INGRID KRAMER
East Germany (1943)

As Miss Kramer in 1960, she became the first non-American winner of the women's Olympic springboard diving title and completed a golden double in the highboard event. Four years later, as Mrs Engel, she successfully defended her springboard championship and took the silver on the highboard. Then in 1968, after a divorce and remarriage, she answered to the name of Mrs Gulbin and finished fifth in her speciality springboard event. She was a double gold medallist in the 1962 European championships and was rated among the top six springboard divers in the world throughout her ten-year international career, which started with a fourth place in the 1958 European championships at the age of fifteen. Noted for her single-minded attitude, she complained that the water in the diving-pool at Tokyo in 1964 was too cold and insisted on taking a hot shower between each dive while on her way to retaining her Olympic springboard crown.

VLADIMIR KUTS
USSR (1927-1975)

A former amateur boxer in the Russian marines, Vladimir Kuts took his aggressive attitude on to the track with him when he switched to athletics at the relatively late age of twenty-two. He competed with the intensity of a man trying to make up for lost time, and he used to run his opponents into the ground with a bold, catch-me-if-you-can style similar to that of Emil Zatopek, whom he succeeded as Olympic 5000 and 10,000 metres champion. Kuts won his two gold medals in Melbourne in 1956, when his front-running tactics drew the sting out of his great British rivals Gordon Pirie, Chris Chataway and Derek

Ibbotson. He twice lost memorable races and his 5000 metres world record to first Chataway in 1954 and then Pirie in 1956. But he got his revenge in the Olympics when it really mattered and just before his retirement in 1957 lowered the 5000 metres world record to 13 min 35 sec, which was unbeaten for seven years.

Kuts first 'arrived' as a world power in the 1954 European 5000 metres championship when he ran away from a top-class field that included Zatopek and Chataway. His victory brought him the first of eight world records including 28 min 30.4 sec for 10,000 metres just a month before his triumph in the 1956 Olympics. Known as the 'Iron Man' of the track, he died of a heart-attack at the age of forty-eight.

Vladimir Kuts: the 'Iron Man' of the track

103

LARISSA LATYNINA
USSR (1934)

The first of the great Russian gymnastic heroines, Larissa Latynina had an incredible Olympic record. She won nine gold medals, five silver and four bronze in a memorable twelve-year career that spanned the Games of 1956, 1960 and 1964. Her speciality event was the floor exercises in which her graceful movements and perfected routines won her three successive Olympic titles. She was close to unbeatable even after giving birth to two children and on top of her Olympic medals haul won eight world titles and five European gold medals. A Russian boycott of the 1963 European championships prevented her having an even more glittering collection of medals. Russia's 'First Lady' of the gymnasium retired in 1966 after what was by her skyscraping standards a disappointing world championship when she won 'only' a silver in the team event.

SAMMY LEE
United States (1920)

The son of Korean parents, Sammy Lee was born and brought up in Fresno, California, where he developed into one of the all-time-great divers. He won the highboard championship at the 1948 London Olympics and took the bronze in the springboard event. Four years later he became the first diver to retain the men's highboard title. Following his retirement he became a doctor, and kept in close contact with his sport as a coach. Bob Webster, highboard diving champion in 1960 and 1964, was one of his pupils. Lee was honoured with the Sullivan Award in 1953 as America's outstanding amateur athlete. He is, of course, a member of the US Swimming Hall of Fame.

ERIK LEMMING
Sweden (1880-1930)

Sweden's 'Man with the Golden Arm' set the first of nine world records in the javelin at the age of nineteen. He was a double gold medallist in the London Olympics of 1908, winning the orthodox javelin event and also the freestyle in which competitors could hold the spear in any fashion. He clutched it in the middle with both hands. He retained the orthodox title in the 1912 Games. A remarkable all-rounder, he made his Olympic debut in 1900 when he finished fourth in the pole vault and fifth in the high jump. The javelin was introduced to the Olympic programme at the 'Interim' Games of 1906 when Lemming won with a world record throw. His first world record in 1899 was 161ft 9¾in (49.32m) and his final record throw in 1912 was 204ft 5½in (62.31m).

RAY LEONARD
United States (1956)

'Sugar Ray' Leonard used the 1976 Montreal Olympics as the launching pad for one of the greatest professional boxing careers of modern times. He won the Olympic light-welterweight title as a member of probably the most powerful amateur squad ever assembled. His United States team-mates included the Spinks brothers, Mike and Leon, Howard Davis and John Tate, all of whom became successful in the professional ring. Leonard outpointed classy Cuban Andres Aldama in the final in Montreal and then cashed in on his fame in spectacular fashion. In a 33-fight career, he was beaten just once — a points defeat by Roberto 'Hands of Stone' Duran that he avenged in devastating fashion. He became the undisputed world welterweight champion and won the WBA version of the world light-middleweight championship. A skilful boxer who could throw combinations of punches at what seemed the speed of light, Leonard earned more than $10 million from the ring before an eye injury forced his premature retirement at the age of twenty-six. He has since announced his intention to make a comeback, with a multi-million dollar 'showdown' fight with Marvin Hagler as his motivation.

ERIC LIDDELL
Great Britain (1902-1945)

The Oscar-winning film *Chariots of Fire* belatedly gave Eric Liddell — and his great track rival Harold Abrahams — the fame and recognition their performances in the 1924 Olympics deserved. Born in Tientsin, China, Liddell was the son of a Scottish missionary and his deep religious principles forced him to withdraw from his speciality event, the 100 metres, because the heats were being staged on a Sunday. The gold medal eventually went to Abrahams. Liddell switched his attentions to the 400 metres, a distance at which he was inexperienced. He astonished everybody (including himself) by winning the final in a world record 47.6 sec, clinging on to a five metre lead that he built up in the first 200 metres covered in an unofficial 22.2 sec. Two days earlier he had taken the bronze medal in the 200 metres in 21.9 sec, with Abrahams sixth in 22.3 sec. Before the Olympics Liddell had never beaten 49 seconds in a one-lap race. He was capped seven times as a Scottish Rugby wing three-quarter before returning to China as a missionary. The man who devoted his life to others tragically died in a Japanese internment camp in China six months before the end of the Second World War. He was forty-three.

JAMES LIGHTBODY
United States (1882-1953)

A Philadelphia-born American with Scottish ancestry, James Lightbody stepped up from the sprints shortly before the 1904 Olympics and quickly established himself as an outstanding middle-distance runner. Competing on the oval-shaped one and a half lap track in St Louis, he won the 800 and 1500 metres, the 2500 metres steeplechase and finished second in the four-mile team race as a representative of Chicago Athletic. He came second in the 800 and won the 1500 metres in the 1906 'Interim' Games in Athens and two years later in London just failed to qualify for the final of the 1500 metres. A feature of his running was a powerful finish in which he used the speed he had built up during two years as a top-flight sprinter.

HARRY LLEWELLYN
Great Britain (1911)
Lt-Col Harry Llewellyn and his horse, Foxhunter, became national heroes when they clinched Britain's only gold medal of the 1952 Olympics in the very last event of the Games. They needed a clear round to give Britain victory in the Prix de Nations equestrian team championship after Wilf White on Nizefela had brought the title within range with a four-fault second round. Llewellyn, who had slept side by side with Foxhunter in the stable before the final round started, coaxed his favourite mount to a brilliant clear round to add a gold medal to the bronze they had collected in 1948. Together they won seventy-eight international competitions including three victories in the King George V Gold Cup. Llewellyn had first concentrated on national hunt racing and finished second in the 1936 Grand National on Ego while still a student at Cambridge University. Following his retirement, he became chairman and later President of the British Show Jumping Association and an influential member of the Sports Council for Wales.

ANITA LONSBROUGH
Great Britain (1941)
Showing the grit and determination typical of her Yorkshire background, Anita Lonsbrough became the only champion to win a swimming gold medal in the 1960 Rome Olympics in a world record time. She clocked 2 min 49.5 sec in the 200 metres breaststroke final to beat red-hot race favourite Wiltrud Urselmann by half a second. Anita deliberately trailed the German for three and a half lengths before unleashing a winning spurt over the last twenty-five metres. In 1962 she realized her ambition of emulating Judy Grinham's feat of completing the swimming 'Grand Slam' of Olympic, Commonwealth and European titles. Anita was seventeen before establishing herself as an international prospect after switching from freestyle to breaststroke. Over the next seven years the popular Huddersfield girl accumulated seven gold medals, three silver and two bronze and was voted Britain's Sportswoman of the Year in 1960 and again in 1962. She retired after competing in the 1964 Tokyo Olympics and married leading professional pursuit cyclist Hugh Porter. She is a regular contributor to BBC radio as a swimming commentator.

Anita Lonsbrough: completed the swimming 'grand slam'

Spiridon Louis: the first great Olympic hero

SPIRIDON LOUIS
Greece (1871-?)
The first great Olympic hero, Spiridon Louis was feted and regaled like a modern Greek god after he had won the marathon at the revival of the Olympic Games in Athens in 1896. It had become a point of national honour that a Greek should win a race that had its roots in Greek legendary history. The trail of the race led from the plain of Marathon to Athens following the course that messenger Pheidippides was said to have run with news of a Greek victory over invading Persian forces in 490 B.C. He dropped down dead in the town centre after proclaiming, 'Rejoice, we conquer.' Louis, a former Greek shepherd who had become a post office messenger after army service, lived to enjoy his fame and a small fortune. All sorts of inducements had been offered to encourage a Greek victory and Louis was one of twenty-one Greek starters in a field of twenty-five. Among the prizes he won were a lifetime's free supply of clothes, wine, chocolate, bread, shaves and haircuts, plus gifts of cattle, sheep and jewellery. His winning time was 2 hr 58 min 50 sec and he was the only man to finish the 25-mile course inside three hours. The one prize he turned down was the offer of the hand of a wealthy benefactor's daughter in marriage for the Greek who could win the race. Louis was already a married man with two children.

JACK LOVELOCK
New Zealand (1910-1949)
Jack Lovelock was the first of the great New Zealand milers to strike gold in the Olympics, Peter Snell and John Walker later following in his famous footsteps. Lovelock won the 1500 metres final in the 1936 Berlin Olympics in devastating fashion. American Glenn Cunningham, the 'Iron Horse of Kansas', tried to burn off all the opposition with his familiar front-running tactics but he and the rest of a top-class field had no answer when Lovelock kicked for home off the first bend of the final lap. He covered the last 300 metres in 42.8 sec to reach the tape in 3 min 47.8 sec for a new world record and what he described in his personal diary as 'the most perfectly executed race of my career.'

'The Man in Black' — as he became known because of his black New Zealand vest and shorts — first revealed that he was a runner out of the ordinary when competing for the combined Cambridge-Oxford university team at Princeton in 1933. He ran away from leading American Bill Bonthron to win the mile event in a world record 4 min 7.6 sec. He then stepped out of the spotlight to concentrate on his medical studies, first at Oxford and later at London Hospital. In his rare appearances before the 1936 Olympics he won a 'Mile of the Century' in Los Angeles and won two and lost two close contests with Britain's Sydney Wooderson, who failed to make the 1500 metres final in 1936 because of a foot injury. His victory in Berlin was a triumph for tactics and planning. He had made up his mind after finishing ninth in the 1932 Olympic 1500 metres final to put all his thoughts and effort into winning the gold medal four years later. In his diary Lovelock stressed that in his opinion an athlete could produce only two peak performances in a season and he planned to perfection so that one of those peaks coincided with the staging of the Berlin Olympics.

Lovelock retired at the end of the 1936 season to devote all his time to his career as a doctor. Four years later he was seriously injured in a fall from a horse and the bang he received on the head affected his eyesight. He died tragically in New York in 1949 when he fell under a train at Church Avenue Station. His name lives on in world athletics as the first of the great Master Milers from New Zealand.

DOUGLAS LOWE
Great Britain (1902-1981)
Douglas Lowe cemented his name in the Olympic record books by becoming the first man to retain the 800 metres title. His first victory came in Paris in 1924 while he was a law student at Cambridge University. He was unfancied for the title because he had never managed to win an AAA championship and it was his team-mate, Henry Stallard, who was expected to lead Britain's challenge for the gold medal. However, Lowe had the speed and the stamina to overtake

Switzerland's highly rated Paul Martin in a neck and neck duel down the finishing straight as Stallard, handicapped by a foot injury, faded to fourth position. He finished fourth in the 1500 metres final. Four years later Lowe repeated his 800 metres triumph in an Olympic record 1 min 51.8 sec after outfoxing a top-class field with a perfectly judged finishing burst. A few weeks later in Berlin he ran the final and fastest race of his career, avenging a previous defeat by Germany's Dr Otto Peltzer with a time of 1 min 51.2 sec. Manchester-born Lowe was secretary of the AAA for seven years in the 1930s before concentrating full-time on his law career.

JANIS LUSIS
USSR (1939)
Janis Lusis, one of the greatest javelin-throwers of all time, has a full set of Olympic medals — a gold in 1968, a silver in 1972 and a bronze in 1964. Further evidence to support Russian claims that he is one of the Great Untouchables of athletics is that he is the only man in any event to have won four successive European titles — 1962, 1966, 1969 and 1971. He became the first Russian to hold the javelin world record in June 1968, when he reached 301 ft 9 in, which was only the second time that the 300 foot barrier had been beaten. A former top-class de-cathlete, Lusis wound down his distinguished career in the 1976 Montreal Games with a creditable eighth place. He is married to Elvira Ozolina, who was the women's Olympic javelin gold medallist in 1960.

PAT McCORMICK
United States (1930)
The wife of an airline pilot, Pat McCormick's career as a diver took off in 1949 when she won the first of seventeen United States titles. She was equally proficient off the springboard or the high board and became the first diver, male or female, to pull off a double championship victory at two successive Olympics. Between her dual triumphs in the 1952 and 1956 Olympics she gave birth to a son. One of the first stars elected to the US Swimming Hall of Fame, Pat became a respected coach in her native California at the end of her remarkable competitive career.

HELENE MADISON
United States (1913)
One of the finest of all pre-war freestyle swimmers, Helene Madison created twenty-two world records in her short three-year career before retiring after a triple gold splash in the 1932 Olympics in Los Angeles. Helene, the 'Seattle Streak', set world records from 100 yards to one mile, and twenty of the records came within an astonishing eighteen-month span. She was the first woman to swim 100 yards in sixty seconds flat and several of her records lasted until the 1940s. Helene was unbeatable in the 1932 Olympics. She became the first woman to win both the 100 and 400 metres and then anchored the United States 4 x 100 metres relay squad to victory in a new world record.

BRONISLAW MALINOWSKI
Poland (1951-1981)
The son of a Polish father and Scottish mother, Bronislaw Malinowski produced one of the great tactical triumphs of the 1980 Olympics when he outfoxed Filbert Bayi to win the 3000 metres steeple-chase after the Tanzanian had threatened to run away with the race. Malinowski had made a name for himself as a front runner, tactics that brought him a silver medal in the steeplechase in the 1976 Games after a fourth place in 1972. He had been a prominent steeplechaser from the age of eighteen after winning the European junior championship but it was not until he was twenty-nine that he collected the major prize for which he had worked so hard. In the Moscow final he was content to sit and bide his time, letting the inexperienced Bayi set a suicidal pace that at one stage had him 35 metres in the lead. Malinowski kept his nerve and relied on his pace judgment; over the last lap he whittled down Bayi's lead and overtook his exhausted rival just before the water jump to go on to a magnificent victory in 8 min 0.9 sec. Tragically, the immensely likeable and highly respected Malinowski was killed in a car crash the following year. It was a sad loss for world athletics.

HARRY MALLIN
Great Britain (1892-1969)
Harry Mallin had the distinction of going through his entire amateur boxing career without a single defeat and his impressive title collection from more than 200 contests included two Olympic gold medals and five successive ABA championships. A London policeman, Mallin was adjudged to have been beaten just once in his career but the decision was reversed in extraordinary circumstances. The judges awarded Frenchman Roger Brousse a disputed points decision over Mallin in their 1924 Olympic middleweight quarter-final contest. A Swedish member of the International Olympic Committee watched the bout from a ringside seat and saw Brousse bite Mallin on the chest. (This was before gumshields were in common use.) Mallin was summoned to a medical examination and as teeth-marks were clearly discerni-ble on his chest the Frenchman was disqualified and the stylish British boxer went on to retain the title he had won in Antwerp four years earlier. When Harry retired his younger brother Fred took up where he left off and won five successive ABA middleweight titles.

Bob Mathias: 'Superman' of the decathlon

BOB MATHIAS
United States (1930)

'Superboy' was one of the labels hung on Bob Mathias after he had won the decathlon gold medal at the 1948 Olympics at the age of seventeen. Four years later the sports scribes promoted him to 'Superman' after he had retained his title with a world record points haul. His victory in London — achieved in only his third decathlon, and against thirty-four of the world's top decathletes — made him the youngest ever gold medallist in Olympic track and field. He was so exhausted as he clinched the title at around midnight on the second day of competition that he vowed he would never compete in another decathlon. Standing 6ft 3 in and weighing 217 lb, Mathias changed his mind and in 1950 set the first of his decathlon world records in his home-town of Tulare, California, where as a boy he had been told to take up sports as a boost to his fight against anaemia. He won all ten decathlons in which he competed, conceding his amateur status in 1953 to star in a Hollywood film based on his life story. Mathias was later elected a Republican Congressman.

RANDY MATSON
United States (1945)

This giant Texan, standing 6ft 6 in and weighing more than eighteen stone, was the first man to beat the 70-foot barrier in the shot-put. He set a world record of 70 ft 7¼ in in 1965 and two years later increased it by an astonishing margin of thirty inches. He had beaten the 60-foot mark while still at high school in 1963 and the following year took the silver medal behind his team-mate Dallas Long in the Tokyo Olympics. Matson was a mighty all-rounder and held the American discus record during 1967. He became Olympic shot-put champion in Mexico in 1968 with a heave of 67ft 4¾in. Noted for his speed across the circle and for the mortar-like explosiveness of his release, Matson set a new Olympic record of 67ft 10¼in in the qualifying round.

ROLAND MATTHES
East Germany (1950)

Roland Matthes dominated men's backstroke swimming for a span of seven years, winning gold medals in the 100 and 200 metres at both the 1968 and 1972 Olympics. His crowns were taken from him in Montreal in 1976 by American John Naber but by then Matthes — a bronze medallist in the 100 metres final — was assured of a permanent place in the Olympic record books. He was a relay specialist and won two silvers and a bronze with the East German team. Coached at the Turbine Club of Erfurt by a woman, Marlies Grohe, Matthes was a brilliant all-rounder who set European records for the 100 metres butterfly and the 200 metres individual medley and was one of East Germany's leading front-crawl swimmers.

KEN MATTHEWS
Great Britain (1934)

The winner of seventeen British walking titles from two miles to twenty miles, Ken Matthews was the king of the road in the 1960s. His greatest triumph came in the 1964 Olympics in Tokyo when he 'walked away' with the 20 kilometres title, crossing the finishing line more than half a minute ahead of his nearest rival. This made up for his bitter disappointment in the 1960 Rome Olympics when he paid for setting too fast a pace in scorching hot conditions, dropping out at the halfway stage in a state of exhaustion. The tall Midlander from Birmingham was an outstanding stylist and never once bothered the judges on the look-out for the feet-off-the-ground 'runners.' He won three other major international championships — the European title in 1962 and the Lugano Trophy (the world team championship) in 1961 and 1963.

RICHARD MEADE
Great Britain (1938)

A brilliant horseman, Richard Meade became Britain's first individual equestrian gold medallist in the 1972 Munich Olympics. His magnificent riding aboard Laurieston lifted Great Britain into first place in the three-day team event, retaining the title he had helped them win four years earlier in Mexico. He made his Olympic debut in 1964 and was leading at one stage but dropped back to eighth after an unhappy experience in the show-jumping ring. He finished fourth in Mexico and fourth again in Montreal in 1976 after completing a clear cross-country round for the fourth Olympic Games in a row, all on different horses. Born in Chepstow, Meade first started riding almost as soon as he could walk at the Connemara Stud run by his parents. He was commissioned into the 11th Hussars before reading engineering at Cambridge.

ALEKSANDR MEDVED
USSR (1937)

Aleksandr Medved cemented his reputation as the greatest freestyle wrestler of all time when he won the super-heavyweight title in Munich in 1972 to complete a historic hat-trick of Olympic gold medals. He then announced his retirement, to close a career unequalled in his sport. Medved was unbeaten in any major competition and the only time he lost a title match was in the 1965 world championships when he was held to a draw by Ahmer Ayik, of Turkey, who took the gold medal on a 'bad marks' count back. The most remarkable thing about Medved was that he never weighed more than seventeen stone but outwrestled opponents who were often ten stone heavier. He took the light-heavyweight title at the 1964 Games and the heavyweight crown four years later in Mexico. His peak performance came in the

Richard Meade: a brilliant horseman

super-heavyweight division in Munich when he used all his speed, strength and guile to master giant thirty-stone American champion Chris Stone.

PIETRO MENNEA
Italy (1952)
It was his storming finish in the outside lane in the 200 metres final in the 1980 Moscow Olympics that robbed flying Scot Allan Wells of a double gold sprint triumph. This was a fitting finale to Mennea's long search for gold. He is the only sprinter in history to win an individual sprint title in his third Olympics. He had taken the bronze medal in 1972 and finished fourth in 1976 and his long-running record gives strength to Italian arguments that he is the finest 200 metre runner of any time. A Bachelor of Political Science, the slim, stylish Mennea had broken Tommie Smith's eleven-year-old 200 metres world record with a 19.72 sec victory in the World Student Games in the thin air of Mexico City in 1979. A month after his Olympic triumph he again beat the 20-second barrier when he clocked 19.96 sec in his native Barletta. He has clocked under 20.30 sec more than twenty times and he has collected three European gold medals and set a European record for 100 metres at 10.01 sec.

DEBBIE MEYER
United States (1952)
Californian schoolgirl Debbie Meyer shook off the handicap of a virus infection to create Olympic history in the swimming pool at the 1968 Games in Mexico City. She won the 200, 400 and 800 metres freestyle titles to become the first swimmer, male or female, to win three individual titles at the same Games. Coached by Sherman Chavoor at the famous Arden Hills club, Maryland-born Debbie created sixteen world records between 1967 and 1970 and had the distinction of being named 'Woman Athlete of the Year' by the Russian news agency Tass after winning the 400 and 800 metres in the 1967 Pan American Games in world record times and at the age of fourteen. She set three world records in the 1968 US Olympic trials but she was not at her peak in Mexico because of a stomach upset, although she still managed to look in a class of her own. Debbie retired in 1970 after just three years of top-flight competition.

ROD MILBURN
United States (1950)
The first man to clock 13.0 sec dead for the 120 yards hurdles, Rod Milburn was a high hurdler with thoroughbred talent. He gave notice of his arrival as a world power in 1971 with twenty-eight consecutive victories including his 13.0 sec run that at last lowered the eleven-year-old record of 13.2 sec set by West Germany's Martin Lauer. He only scraped into

the American team for the 1972 Games with a third place in the US Olympic trials but he was back to peak form in Munich. Milburn glided over the barriers to take the gold medal in a world record for 110 metres hurdles of 13.24 sec. He lowered the world record to 13.1 sec in 1973 before turning professional. Reinstated as an amateur in 1980, he quickly proved he was still a force to be reckoned with as he hurdled to a series of victories in world-class times.

BILLY MILLS
United States (1938)
A lieutenant in the US Marines, Billy Mills helped launch America's explosion of interest in distance running when he won the 10,000 metres on the first day of the 1964 Olympics in Tokyo. The United States had never before won the 5000 or 10,000 metres in the history of the Olympics and the success of Mills inspired his countryman Bob Schulz to make it a double by winning the 5000. Mills, a descendant of American Indians, shadowed Australian race favourite Ron Clarke in the 10,000 metres and then revealed stunning finishing speed to outsprint multi-world record holder Clarke and Tunisian Mohamed Gammoudi. His winning time was an Olympic record 28 min 24.4 sec, an improvement on his previous personal best of forty-five seconds.

ALAIN MIMOUN
France (1921)
This French-Algerian — born Ali Mimoun O'Kacha — recovered from a war wound received in the battle of Cassino to become one of the world's running masters. He spent much of his career running in the footsteps of the immortal Emil Zatopek, collecting a silver medal behind him in the 10,000 metres in the 1948 Olympics and again in the 5000 and 10,000 metres in the 1952 Games. The galloping Czech also beat him into second place in two European championship races but Mimoun shook off his Zatopek complex in the 1956 Olympics in Melbourne when he won the marathon in 2 hours 25 minutes, just outside the Olympic record set by Zatopek four years earlier. The defending champion finished sixth and waiting to hug him as he crossed the line was his old friend and rival Alain Mimoun. Just a year earlier Mimoun — a king of cross-country running — had been hobbling around with the aid of a stick because of a recurring foot injury. He nevertheless vowed to run his first marathon in Melbourne and there was no more popular or deserving champion than the tall, shuffling Frenchman.

RUSSELL MOCKRIDGE
Australia (1930-1958)
One of the most versatile cyclists ever to compete at

6world level, Russell Mockridge made his Olympic debut in London in 1948 when — after a series of punctures — he finished twenty-sixth in the 101 mile road race. The bespectacled Australian, who had studied for the Church, won two gold medals in Helsinki four years later when he showed his strength and speed in winning the 1000 metres time trial and the 2000 metres tandem in partnership with Lionel Cox. He was selected for the 1952 Olympics only after being forced by the Australian cycling authorities to sign an agreement that he would not turn professional for at least a year. Mockridge joined the European professional tour after winning ten Australian sprint championships and proving himself the king of the road as well as the track Down Under. He completed the Tour de France in 1955 and in the same year partnered another great Australian cycling hero, Sid Patterson, to victory in the Paris six-day race. Mockridge died tragically in 1958 following a crash while competing in a road race in his native Melbourne.

DANIEL MORELON
France (1944)
Daniel Morelon failed by inches to complete a hat-trick of gold medals in the 1000 metres sprint in the Olympic cycling championships in Montreal in 1976. Czech ace Anton Tkac swooped past him with a beautifully judged finish to take his title, as he had done two years earlier in the world championships. But the defeats could not dent Morelon's reputation as one of the quickest and smoothest sprint cyclists ever to sit in the saddle. He had taken the bronze medal in 1964 and then captured the gold in 1968 and 1972. Often timed at speeds over 40 mph, Morelon teamed up with his famous countryman Pierre Trentin to win the 2000 metres tandem title in Mexico in 1968. His greatest asset apart from his speed was a calculating tactical mind and he continually lured opponents into the trap of thinking they had him beaten, only to produce a sudden acceleration that would carry him to victory.

BOBBY JOE MORROW
United States (1935)
The first Texan track and field athlete to win a post-war Olympic championship, Bobby Joe Morrow swept impressively to a golden hat-trick in the 1956 Games in Melbourne. He was never headed throughout the Games, winning his four rounds and final of the 100 metres and then completing the double in the 200 metres despite a heavily strapped thigh following a slight muscle-pull. Morrow — as great a white sprinter as ever ran — anchored the United States sprint relay team to victory on the final day of the championships when he forced his 6ft 1½in frame through the tape in a new world record 39.5 sec. A joint world record holder at 100 yards, 100 metres and 200 metres, Morrow first established himself as a top-flight sprinter while studying at Abilene Christian College, where he was also an outstanding gridiron footballer. His defeats between 1955 and 1959 could be counted on the fingers of one hand, and he put his mind to becoming the first sprinter to retain an Olympic title. However, his preparations were handicapped by injury and he just failed to make the 1960 US Olympic team after clocking 20.8 sec in the trials. He is now a respected coach.

JOHN NABER
United States (1955)
It was impossible not to notice John Naber during the 1976 Olympic swimming championships in Montreal. He stood a lanky 6ft 6in, wore a woollen scarf decorated with badges and clowned around so much at the pool-side that his team-mates nicknamed him 'Fruit Cake'. Naber also stood out in the water because of his great talent. He won gold medals in both backstroke events and became the first man to break the two-minute barrier in the 200 metres event with a world record clocking of 1 min 59.19 sec. A third-year student of psychology at the University of Southern California, Naber was versatile as well as powerful in the water and he collected gold medals in the medley and freestyle relays and finished second in the 200 metres freestyle.

NEDO NADI
Italy (1893-1940)
Italy has produced a procession of outstanding fencing champions but none quite in the class of Nedo Nadi, a supreme master of his sport. The son of Beppe Nadi — one of the world's foremost fencers at the turn of the century — Nedo was fencing before he was out of short trousers and by his late teens had a technical excellence with all the weapons that only the most experienced fencers could match. He won the foil event at the 1912 Stockholm Olympics and then served in the Italian Army in the First World War when he was decorated for his bravery in action. His peak performances came in the 1920 Olympics in Stockholm where he won individual titles at foil and sabre and led the Italian team to victory in all three classifications for a record haul of five gold medals. His brother, Aldo, was a silver medallist in the sabre and won three team golds. Nedo went to Argentina as a professional instructor but returned to Italy, where he was reinstated as an amateur and became president of the Italian fencing federation, a post he held at the time of his death during the Second World War.

IMRE (1921) and MIKLOS NEMETH (1946)
Hungary
Miklos Nemeth was twenty months old when his

Miklos Nemeth was twenty months old when his father, Imre, became the Olympic hammer-throwing champion at the 1948 London Olympics. Imre hurled the hammer 183ft 11½in (56.07m) to win Hungary's first gold medal in Olympic athletics since 1900. Three times a world record holder in the 1940s, Imre encouraged his son to concentrate on athletics in his native Budapest and he emerged as a fine all-rounder. Miklos was a promising long-jumper but decided to devote all his energies to the javelin event after he had started to produce world-class throws at the age of twenty. For ten years Nemeth jnr was one of the leading throwers in Europe but his mediocre performances in the major championships suggested he had not inherited his father's competitive qualities. Miklos finally silenced his critics and stepped out of his father's shadow with his very first throw in the 1976 Montreal Olympics when he sent the javelin soaring to a world record 310ft 3 in (94.58m). It was the throw of a lifetime for Miklos, who was never able to repeat it and slipped to eighth in defence of his crown in the 1980 Moscow Games. But he could retire happy in the knowledge that the Nemeth name was part of Olympic history.

MARTHA NORELIUS
United States (1908-1955)
Stockholm-born Martha Norelius was the first woman swimmer to win an Olympic gold medal for the same event at successive Olympics. The daughter of Swedish international swimmer Charles Norelius, Martha was brought up in the United States where she was coached first by her father and then by the famous New York champion-maker Louis de B. Handley. She won the 400 metres freestyle in the 1924 Games in Paris and then retained the title in Amsterdam four years later with a time of 5 min 42.8 sec, one of nineteen world records she set before touring the world as a professional. Martha won a third gold medal as a member of the American 4 x 100 metres freestyle relay team. In 1929 she won the $10,000 Wrigley ten-mile challenge race in Toronto where she met and married Canadian Olympic sculler Joe Wright.

PAAVO NURMI
Finland (1897-1973)
'Peerless' Paavo Nurmi left behind footprints that will be permanent in running history. Nine Olympic gold medals (six individual and three in team races) and twenty-two world records tell the statistical story of why he was a legend in his own lifetime. What his honours haul does not reveal is that he was the first great personality performer of athletics, a true superstar of the track who pulled massive crowds wherever he ran. He was inspired as a youngster by the running exploits of the 'Father of the Flying Finns', Hannes Kolehmainen, and succeeded his idol as

Paavo Nurmi: an indomitable force

10,000 metres and cross-country champion at the 1920 Olympics in Antwerp. He collected a silver medal in the 5000 metres behind Joseph Guillemot but got his revenge over the Frenchman in the 10,000 metres.

Nurmi set the first of his world records over six miles in 1921 and his last over two miles ten years later. He was an indomitable force in the Paris Games of 1924, finishing first in seven races in six days which included Olympic records and gold medals in the 1500 and 5000 metres on the same afternoon and with less than ninety minutes between them. Nurmi, who usually ran with a stopwatch in his hand to perfect his pace, recaptured the 10,000 metres title in the 1928 Olympics and was a silver medallist in the 5000 and 3000 metres steeplechase, an event at which he was a virtual novice. He became a globetrotting, 'have-spikes-will-travel' champion and won all but two of sixty-eight races on the United States circuit. His plan to wind down his astonishing Olympic career in the marathon in Los Angeles in 1932 was destroyed on the eve of the Games when he was banned for alleged professionalism. He continued running in his homeland until the age of thirty-six and made a nostalgic return to the Olympic arena in 1952 when he and his hero Hannes Kolehmainen carried out the traditional flame-lighting ceremony at Helsinki, in which city there stands a bronze statue of Nurmi as a lasting tribute to a giant of athletics.

PARRY O'BRIEN
United States (1932)

Justifiably known as the 'Big Shot' of athletics, Parry O'Brien was Olympic shot-put champion in 1952 and 1956, the silver medallist in 1960 and finished fourth in 1964. He revolutionized the style of shot-putting with a step-back technique in which he started his build-up to the throw with his back to the point of release. At first his rivals ridiculed his new method but then hastily copied it as he put together a sequence of 116 victories and raised the world record fourteen times. A great believer in the merits of weight training, O'Brien was a top-class all-rounder who was a sub-11 sec 100 metre runner and America's discus champion in 1955. The Californian competed at top level for nineteen seasons and had the distinction of being the first man to beat the sixty-foot, eighteen-metre and nineteen-metre barriers. The style he introduced continues to be used by most of the world's leading shot-putters and helped his immediate successors Bill Neider, Dallas Long and Randy Matson carry on America's supremacy in the powerman event.

PAT O'CALLAGHAN
Eire (1906)

Just a year after taking up hammer-throwing as his speciality event, Irish doctor Pat O'Callaghan won the Olympic title at the 1928 Games in Amsterdam with a throw of 168ft 7in — an improvement of more than thirty feet on his first ever throw twelve months earlier. O'Callaghan was like a one-man field events team, as he proved in 1931 when winning six Irish championships, including the discus, shot and high jump. He retained his Olympic title in Los Angeles in 1932 with his last throw after trailing in second place for most of the competition. International politics prevented him defending his title at Berlin in 1936 but the following year he produced the longest throw of his career — 195ft 5in (59.56m). It beat Irish-American Patrick Ryan's 24-year-old world record by six feet but failed to get international recognition because the hammer was found to be six ounces overweight and the throwing circle six inches too small.

AL OERTER
United States (1936)

Al Oerter well merited his nickname 'The Man with the Golden Arm' by winning four successive gold medals in the discus, one for each of his four children. His extraordinary competitive powers were best illustrated in the 1964 Tokyo Games when he completed his hat-trick despite being doubly handicapped by the pain of a pinched nerve in his back and a torn rib cartilage. Standing 6ft 4in and weighing 260 lb, Oerter won his first gold medal at the 1956 Games in Melbourne when a twenty-year-old outsider and just two years after breaking the American high school record. He made it a unique four triumphs in a row at Mexico in 1968 with a lifetime's best throw of 212ft 5in (64.78m). The New York-born computer programme analyst broke the world record four times and made a comeback at forty with a fifth gold medal in mind, a dream that died with America's boycott of the Moscow Olympics.

Al Oerter: four successive gold medals

HAROLD OSBORN
United States (1899)

The Olympics brought Harold Osborn romance as well as the unique distinction of being the only decathlon champion to also win a title in an individual event. A bespectacled all-rounder from Butler, Illinois, Osborn won the high jump in the 1924 Games in Paris with a leap of 6ft 6in (1.98m) and then five days later clinched the decathlon gold medal with a then world record haul of 7710 points. He failed to retain his high-jump title in Amsterdam four years later but found himself a wife — Canada's winner of the women's Olympic high-jump gold medal, Ethel Calderwood. Osborn, a skilled osteopath, won eighteen US national titles in six different events and at the age of thirty-seven set a new world standing high-jump record of 5ft 6in (1.68m). Some of his high-jumping rivals referred to him as 'the crafty champion' because he perfected the art of pressing down and steadying the bar against the uprights as he made his clearance. There was so much controversy over his technique that the rules were changed in 1927 so that the bar had to be placed in such a way that it could fall either forward or backward.

MICHELINE OSTERMEYER
France (1922)

A prize-winning classical pianist at the Paris Conservatoire, Micheline Ostermeyer used her hands to fine effect in the Olympic field events in London in 1948. She won the shot, her speciality event, and then amazed herself as much as her team-mates by also winning the discus, in which she was a virtual novice. For good measure, Micheline additionally collected a bronze medal in the high-jump. At a celebration party at the French hotel headquarters Micheline gave another winning performance — this time at the piano keyboard with an impromptu Beethoven recital.

STEVE OVETT
Great Britain (1955)

Steve Ovett impressively regained his world 1500 metres world record in the summer of 1983 to prove he still has the speed and the motivation to capture the gold medal that eluded him in the 1980 Olympics. He went to Moscow as favourite to win the 1500 metres title, with his gifted compatriot Sebastian Coe expected to give him a close race. Coe was the hot tip for the 800 metres gold. These two great rivals both became Olympic champions but not in the way everybody had been predicting. Ovett revealed he could mix it with the best of them when he won a physically punishing 800 metres final, with Coe picking up a silver medal at the end of a race in which he admitted his tactics were almost novice-like. It looked odds-on a golden double for the supremely confident Ovett who went into the 1500 metres final with a string of 45 consecutive mile and metric mile victories behind him. But Coe wiped out the nightmare memory of his performance in the 800 metres with the run of a lifetime, taking the lead off the final bend and going away to win in magnificent style. The outgunned Ovett had to make do with a bronze medal behind East German Jurgen Straub. Both Coe and Ovett are articulate and intelligent characters and rate as two of the finest athletes ever to set foot on the running track. Together they have given British athletics a tremendous boost. Ovett, a Brighton art student before switching full time to athletics, is coached by Harry Wilson and is a born racer who loves the challenge of competition, whether it is at club or internaional level. He has been the world record holder at the mile as well as the 1500 metres and although having to race in Steve Cram's footsteps in 1983 he is certain to be a force to be reckoned with in Los Angeles.

JESSE OWENS
United States (1913-1980)

Just one afternoon in the life of Jesse Owens can be used to illustrate why he is a track and field immortal. Competing in a universities championship meet at Ann Arbor, Michigan, on 25 May, 1935, he beat or equalled six world records in just a fraction over forty-five minutes. He ran 100 yards in 9.4 sec; 220 yards in 20.3 sec (collecting the 200 metres world record en route); set new world figures for the hurdles over 220 yards and 200 metres; and took five minutes off from his track commitments to long-jump 26ft 8¼in (8.13m) for a world record that was to survive for a quarter of a century. These prodigious performances alone were enough to assure Owens of lasting fame, but a little over a year later in the 1936 Olympics he gave further mind-blowing evidence that he was an absolutely phenomenal athlete.

He used the Berlin stage (on which Hitler was anticipating a show of Aryan superiority) to reveal Black power at its most devastating. He equalled or lowered no fewer than twelve Olympic records on his way to gold medals in the 100 metres, 200 metres, long-jump and sprint relay and only a following wind fractionally above the permissible limit prevented recognition of a new world record of 10.2 sec for 100 metres. A beautifully balanced and naturally graceful runner, Owens was also a dignified and sporting competitor. He was locked in a compelling duel with German ace Luz Long in the long-jump competition and at the peak of their contest massaged his opponent's cramped leg. Owens trailed Long until the fifth jump and then clinched the gold medal with

Following pages
Steve Ovett: two-lap winner in Moscow

Jesse Owens: a track and field immortal

the first clearance in the Olympics of 26 feet and then reached 26ft 5¼in (8.06m) with his final jump for a Games record that lasted until 1960. One of eight children of an Alabama cotton-picker, James Cleveland Owens became universally known as Jesse because of his initials J.C. He was motivated as a youngster by the 1920 Olympic victory of sprinter Charley Paddock, just as he himself was to inspire 1948 champion Harrison Dillard. Owens ran a wind-aided 100 metres in 10.3 sec at the age of eighteen, and in the same season long-jumped to within a fraction of 25 feet. This earned him an athletics scholarship to Ohio State University where coach Larry Snyder gave him technique to go with his awesome natural talent. He became something of a travelling sideshow after the Berlin Olympics, touring with the Harlem Globetrotters as a professional and running against racehorses. However, his great dignity was restored after the war when he started working for underprivileged children and he was invited to attend major championships around the world as a popular VIP. The United States has never had a better sporting ambassador. He died in the Olympic year of 1980 but his name will live on for ever in sports history. Jesse Owens would have a lot of support in the debate as to who has been the athlete of the century.

ANN PACKER
Great Britain (1942)

Ann Packer went to the 1964 Tokyo Olympics as one of the favourites for the 400 metres title and returned home as gold medallist and world record holder for 800 metres. Originally a sprinter, hurdler and long-jumper, fleet and lovely Ann had run only five competitive two-lap races before the Games in which she took a silver medal in her speciality 400 metres event behind Australia's 'beaut' Betty Cuthbert. Three days later she lined up as an outsider in the 800 metres final and produced an incredible finishing kick off the final bend to outsprint the Eastern European favourites. She crossed the line in a world record 2 min 0l.1 sec and ran into the arms of British team captain Robbie Brightwell, then her fiancé and now her husband. It was Ann's last major race and she retired to become a wife and mum. Even now, twenty years later, she still has the satisfaction of knowing her winning time in Tokyo is faster than most current British women two-lap runners can manage.

Ann Packer: coming on the outside to strike gold

Charley Paddock (extreme left): a 'flying finish'

CHARLEY PADDOCK
United States (1900-1943)
One of the great showmen of the track, 1920s sprint star Charley Paddock used to take the eye of the spectators and the judges with his famous 'flying finish'. He would leap through the tape with arms stretched wide and claimed that the technique was responsible for his stunning sequence of success. Paddock was the 1920 100 metres Olympic champion, silver medallist in the 200 metres and anchored the United States sprint relay squad to victory in a world record 42.2 sec. The thick-set Texan, the first athlete to be labelled 'The World's Fastest Human' and the man who inspired a young Jesse Owens, set or equalled world records eleven times between 1920 and 1924 but with a running style that made coaching purists wince. A French doctor tried to analyse what made Paddock tick and came away shaking his head, saying: 'He is fat, his arms and shoulders are like those that you would find on a middle-aged matron and he runs like a calf with two heads. I would be inclined to tell all young sprinters to do everything opposite to him — yet he is the fastest man on earth!' Paddock finished fifth in the 100 metres in the Paris Olympics behind Harold Abrahams and collected a silver in the 200 metres. He also competed in the 1928 Games but without reaching a final. A captain in the Marines during the Second World War, he was killed in an air crash, but his memory was honoured when a United States battleship was named after him.

LASZLO PAPP
Hungary (1926)
A stylish, hard-hitting southpaw, Laszlo Papp won three successive Olympic gold medals — in 1948 at middleweight and in 1952 and 1956 at light-middleweight. He then became the first 'Iron Curtain' boxer to be permitted to box professionally and he won all his twenty-nine paid contests. The moustachioed Papp won the professional European middleweight title and was lined up for a world title challenge when the Hungarian Government declared that he could no longer box for financial gain. This gifted ring-master hung up his gloves at the age of thirty-eight and became the respected trainer of the Hungarian national team.

FLOYD PATTERSON
United States (1935)
Floyd Patterson was the first Olympic boxing champion to go on to win the sport's peak prize, the professional world heavyweight title. He won the middleweight gold medal in the 1952 Helsinki Olympics, and four years later became at twenty-one years and eleven months the youngest ever winner of the world heavyweight crown when he knocked out Archie Moore in five rounds in a contest for the title vacated by Rocky Marciano. Patterson, a reformed juvenile delinquent from a tough area of Brooklyn, was noted for the speed of his combination punches but because of a lack of height and weight (5ft 11in, 13 st 8 lb) he was never comfortable against the real giants of the ring and was beaten in title fights by Sonny Liston and Muhammad Ali. He created more ring history in 1960 when he became the first heavyweight champion to regain the title, knocking out Ingemar Johansson in five rounds a year after being stopped in three rounds by the heavy-punching Swede. Patterson continues to serve his sport with great dignity as a New York boxing commissioner.

Laszlo Papp: decking Britain's Johnny Wright in 1948

RODNEY PATTISON
Great Britain (1943)

Scotsman Rodney Pattison gave up a Navy career to pursue his yachting interests and became one of the finest small-boat sailors in the world. He teamed up with crewman Iain Macdonald-Smith to win the Flying Dutchman class in *Superdocious* in the 1968 Olympics at Acapulco. They were among the most successful partners in the history of dinghy-racing and their triumph in Mexico was their peak performance during a procession of international victories. The popular British pair overcame the handicap of an early disqualification to win five races in succession and take the gold medal. They underlined their superiority by winning the world championship in 1970 and then decided to go their separate ways. Pattison teamed up with Chris Davies for the 1972 Olympics, this time in *Superdoso*, and again the tactical genius of the Scot shone through as he helmed his boat to victory. He took delivery of his new boat for the 1976 Games only ten weeks before

the competition got under way and, lacking preparation, had to be content with a silver medal, this time with Julian Brooke Houghton as his crewman.

MEL PATTON
United States (1924)

The world record for the 100 yards dash had stood at 9.4 sec for more than eighteen years until Mel Patton finally broke through the 'wall' to record 9.3 sec in May, 1948. Three months later he went to his starting blocks in the Olympic 100 metres final a scorching hot favourite to win but nerves got the better of him and he faded to a disappointing fifth place behind storybook winner Harrison 'Bones' Dillard. Patton, whose entry as a freshman at the University of Southern California had been delayed by wartime service in the US Navy, showed his competitive qualities by producing his best form in the 200 metres final, holding off a strong challenge from team-mate Barney Ewell to win in 21.1 sec on a soaked Wembley track. He completed a hat-trick of medals by helping the United States win the sprint relay. Patton turned professional in 1949 after setting world records for

220 yards and 200 metres and was still a formidable force on the professional circuit some six years later when he produced some storming runs during a tour of Australia.

PASCUAL PEREZ
Argentina (1926)

Standing just 4ft 11in and weighing only a few pounds over seven stone, Pascual Perez packed dynamic punching power that belied his size. Perez overwhelmed Italian champion Spartaco Bandinelli in the final of the flyweight division in the 1948 Olympics in London and then punched his way to even greater fame in the professional ring. The 'Mighty Midget' from Buenos Aires became the first Argentinian boxer to win a world title when he went to Tokyo in 1954 to relieve Japanese Yoshio Shirai of the championship. Perez, who did not join the professional ranks until he was twenty-six, had an unbeaten run of fifty contests and made thirteen successful title defences before losing his crown to Pone Kingpetch, of Thailand, in 1960. He boxed on for another four years, finally retiring at the age of thirty-eight after winning seventy-five of eighty-three professional fights.

MARY PETERS
Great Britain (1939)

There have been few more popular women Olympic champions than Mary Peters, winner of the pentathlon at the 1972 Games in Munich with a world record haul of 4801 points. Mary had lived in the shadow of the multi-talented Mary Rand for much of her seventeen-year athletics career and her fourth place in the 1964 Olympic pentathlon seemed the best she could hope to achieve. But she reached down into her reserves of stamina to find an amazing new peak of performance after gold medals in the 1970 Commonwealth pentathlon and shot-put events had given her fresh motivation. Born in Lancashire but raised in her beloved Belfast, Mary produced a series of inspired displays in all five of the pentathlon disciplines in Munich to hold off the determined challenge of West German favourite Heide Rosendahl. She finally won the gold medal by just ten points and her fitness, dedication and determination at the age of thirty-two were a credit to the stimulating influence of her enthusiastic Northern Ireland coach Buster McShane. Mary continues to serve athletics in an official capacity, and was the Great Britain women's team manager at the 1980 Olympics.

Mary Peters (nearest camera): a peak performance

DORANDO PIETRI
Italy (1885-1942)

Dorando Pietri is the only Olympic hero featured in this section of the book who never won an Olympic gold medal. What he did win was the hearts of a nation as he bravely battled to finish the 1908 London marathon when in a state of complete exhaustion. It is now a permanent part of Olympic legend how Dorando — the name by which he was entered in the official Games programme — staggered into the White City Stadium with just 385 yards between him and the Olympic title. The extra yards had been added to the 26 mile course so that the runners could finish in front of Queen Alexandra's Royal Box. Dorando, a pastrycook from Capri, looked an almost Chaplinesque figure as he tottered into the stadium on weary, spindly legs that were suddenly refusing to obey him. He turned the wrong way as he came off the road on to the track and he was pointed and pushed in the right direction for the tape. Staggering drunkenly from one side of the cinder track to the other, Dorando made it to the finishing line only after well-meaning officials had steered him by the elbow. He collapsed on the track and a doctor had to

massage his heart back into place because it had moved half an inch out of position. Inevitably, Dorando was disqualified because it was decided he had not finished the course under his own steam. New York store clerk John Hayes came in second and was awarded the gold medal. For Dorando there was the consolation of a special gold cup presented to him by Queen Alexandra and lasting fame as a true hero of the Olympics. He later joined the professional running circuit and was prominent in a series of marathon races in the United States.

NINA PONOMARYEVA
USSR (1929)

Gold medals at the 1952 and 1960 Olympics and a bronze in 1956 confirmed Nina Ponomaryeva as the outstanding woman discus-thrower of the 1950s. She won nine successive Russian championships and set a world record of 157ft 6in in 1952 three weeks after her first Olympic victory. In Melbourne in 1960 she became the first woman to win an Olympic field event twice with a Games record throw of 180ft 9½in. Competing in her fourth Olympics in 1964 at the age of thirty-five, she finished eleventh. She was ranked in the top three in the world for eleven consecutive seasons. Nina made headlines for sad reasons during

Dorando Pietri: nearing the end of the road

a trip to Britain with the Russian team in 1956. She was arrested on a shoplifting charge and was given an absolute discharge after being found guilty. It caused a major international incident, Russia cancelling their scheduled match against Britain and Nina hiding out in the Russian embassy in London before finally presenting herself in court after a warrant had been issued for her arrest.

TAMARA (1937) *and* IRINA (1939) PRESS
USSR

The incredible Press sisters between them collected five Olympics gold medals and created a total of twenty-three world records in a span of just six years. Born in the Ukraine, they were lucky to escape with their lives when their parents fled with them from their native city of Kharkov just ahead of invading German troops during the Second World War. Tamara was the first to show athletic prowess, making the shot and discus her speciality events although she was an international-class hurdler. Irina concentrated on the hurdles and developed into an outstanding pentathlete. Tamara won the shot in the 1960 and 1964 Games and took the gold medal and the silver in the discus in the same Olympics. Irina won the 80 metres hurdles in 1960 and the pentathlon four years later. Their international careers came to a controversial end in 1966 when they pulled out of the European championships because, according to official reports, their mother was ill. It was suggested in some quarters that they were withdrawn rather than face the mandatory 'sex test' that was introduced for these championships.

DON QUARRIE
Jamaica (1951)

There is a statue of Don Quarrie in his native Kingston, erected to mark his victory in the 200 metres in the 1976 Olympics in Montreal. He came close to a double, finishing just 1/100th sec behind fellow West Indian Hasley Crawford, of Trinidad, in the 100 metres. Reports of the emergence of Quarrie as a dynamic sprinter started to trickle out of Jamaica two years before he proved the stories true with a 100/200 metres double in the 1970 Commonwealth Games when he was just nineteen. Injury prevented him competing in the 1968 Olympics and a pulled muscle put him out of the 1972 Games after he had reached the semi-final of the 200 metres. Quarrie, who continues to be a popular globetrotting athlete, retained his Commonwealth titles in 1974 and beat Allan Wells in the 100 metres final in 1978. He made a bold defence of his Olympic 200 metres crown in Moscow in 1980, taking the bronze medal behind Pietro Mennea and Wells.

PAUL RADMILOVIC
Great Britain (1886-1968)

As you might expect of somebody born in Cardiff of a Greek father and Irish mother, Paul Radmilovic was one of the most extraordinary characters in British sport in the first quarter of the century. He was a scratch golfer, an international-class amateur footballer and a versatile enough swimmer to win fifteen Welsh 100 yards freestyle titles and nine English championships at distances ranging from 100 yards to five miles. All these were sidelines to his speciality sport of water polo. 'Raddy', who lived for most of his life in Weston-super-Mare, won gold medals with the British water polo team in the 1908, 1912 and 1920 Olympics. He also competed in the 1924 and 1928 Games when, at the age of forty-two, he helped the team to finish fourth. Despite the fact that his peak-power years were lost to the First World War, Raddy amassed the most gold medals ever won by a British competitor. He lifted his collection to four golds as a member of Britain's winning 4 x 200 metres relay team in London in 1908.

MARY RAND
Great Britain (1940)

It was obvious that a true diamond of a prospect had been unearthed when a pretty seventeen-year-old Somerset girl called Mary Bignal set a British pentathlon record of 4046 points in 1957. Seven years later, after marriage to champion sculler Sydney Rand and the birth of a daughter, the early promise was completely fulfilled when Mary won the long-jump gold medal at the Tokyo Olympics with a world record leap of 22ft 2¼in (6.76m). At the same 1964 Games she took the silver medal in the pentathlon and helped the British squad collect a bronze in the sprint relay. The former Millfield schoolgirl had made her Olympics debut in Rome in 1960, finishing fourth in the 80 metres hurdles and ninth in the long jump after leading in the qualifying round. She developed into the greatest all-round athlete in the history of British women's athletics and added to her honours haul in the 1966 Commonwealth Games with a gold medal in the long jump. A muscle injury prevented her defending her Olympic title in 1968 but she attended the Games in Mexico as a TV commentator. A year later, after announcing her retirement from athletics, Mary married for a second time. Her new husband was 1968 Olympic decathlon champion Bill Toomey, with whom she now lives in California.

BOB RICHARDS
United States (1926)

They used to joke on the athletics circuit that Bob Richards took up the pole vault so that he could get closer to God. An ordained minister of the Church of the Brethren, he was known as the 'Vaulting Vicar' and dominated his event for more than a decade. He

Mary Rand: 1964 was her golden leap year

was third in the 1948 Olympics and the gold medallist in 1952 and again in 1956. Richards was at his peak before the introduction of the whippy fibreglass poles and regularly cleared 15 feet with a metal pole that gave nothing like the catapult assistance of today's poles. He used to arrive at meetings straight from delivering sermons with his Bible in one hand and his pole in the other. Richards was also a top-class decathlete and was three times American decathlon champion.

JOHAN RICHTOFF
Sweden (1898)
A seventeen-stone wrestler, Johan Richtoff used speed and intelligent tactics to outmanœuvre opponents who often outweighed him by as much as ten stone. He won the freestyle heavyweight championship in 1928 and retained it four years later in Los Angeles where promoters persuaded him to turn professional as a catch-wrestler on the US tour. He used to make beer barrels as a cooper in a brewery but was later ordained as a minister in the Swedish Free Church and became a campaigner against the evils of alcohol. Richtoff wrestled as a professional in the United States for only a year before returning to the pulpit to preach temperance.

AILEEN RIGGIN
United States (1906)
Aileen Riggin captured the hearts of the American public when at the age of fourteen she became the first women's springboard diving champion at the Antwerp Olympics in 1920. She was the youngest gold medallist in Olympic history until another American, Marjorie Gestring, won the springboard title at the age of thirteen in the 1936 Games. Helen Wainwright, silver medallist behind Aileen in 1920, beat her into second place in the springboard competition in the 1924 Olympics during which Aileen took a bronze medal in the 100 metres backstroke to become the first competitor to win a swimming and diving medal. Idolized in her home-town of Newport, Rhode Island, Aileen toured the world as a professional before starting a career in Hollywood as an adviser and occasional performer in films featuring aquatic sequences.

VILLE RITOLA
Finland (1896)
Ville Ritola is the 'forgotten man' of athletics whose outstanding track performances were continually overshadowed by the superb running of the peerless Paavo Nurmi. Ritola won three individual gold medals, two team golds and three individual silver medals in the 1924 and 1928 Olympics, which in normal circumstances would have guaranteed him a lasting place in any sporting hall of fame. But Ritola

was nearly always having to run in Nurmi's footsteps in the major races. His three silver medals were won behind Nurmi in the 5000 metres and 10,000 metres cross-country event in 1924 and four years later in the track 10,000 metres, the title he had captured in the Paris Games with a world record 30 min 23.2 sec. Just two days after his world record run he set a world's best in the 3000 metres steeplechase. He managed to get the better of the great Nurmi in the 5000 metres in Amsterdam in 1928 but came off second best in five meetings out of six on the American indoor circuit. Ritola spent much of his time in the United States as a prominent member of the Finnish-American track and field club and won fourteen AAU outdoor championships.

GASTON ROELANTS
Belgium (1937)
Gaston — 'The Gastank' — Roelants has proved himself a runner of seemingly limitless stamina since he first started taking a serious interest in athletics back in 1954. After finishing fourth in the 1960 Olympic 3000 metres steeplechase, he failed to win just one of his next forty-eight steeplechase races. His one defeat came in a heat of the 1964 Olympic event and he went on to win the gold medal in an Olympic record 8 min 30.8 sec. In the previous year he had become the first man to break the 8 min 30 sec barrier and in 1965, revealing the bold, front-running style that is his trademark, he lowered the world record to 8 min 26.4 sec. The winner of four International Cross Country Championships, Roelants stepped up to endurance events and in 1966 he set new world records for 20,000 metres, and for covering the greatest distance in one hour. He beat both records six years later. The popular Belgian has clocked 2 hr 16 min 30 sec for the marathon and even in his late forties is rated as one of the world's top marathoners.

MURRAY ROSE
Australia (1939)
Scottish-born Murray Rose emerged as the 'golden boy' of Australian swimming after his family had emigrated Down Under in the immediate post-war years. A devastating exponent of the front crawl, Rose created nine freestyle world records from 400 to 1500 metres and shared in six sprint relay world records with the Australian national team. His peak year was in 1956 when he collected gold medals in the 400 and 1500 metres freestyle and in the 4 x 200 metres relay in the Melbourne Olympics. Four years later in Rome he retained the 400 metres title and took a silver medal behind team-mate Jon Konrads. Rose, a vegetarian and health-food fanatic, became a student at the University of Southern California and his return to Australia for the 1962 Commonwealth Games in Perth was sponsored by a newspaper. He responded by winning four gold medals. The Austra-

lian selectors omitted him from the team for the Tokyo Olympics in 1964 because he could not take time off from his studies to join in the Olympic trials. It was a harsh and blind decision by the selectors in a year in which Rose set two more world records to prove he was still a formidable force.

RALPH ROSE
United States (1884-1913)
If legend is to be believed, this mountain of a man — 6ft 6in tall and weighing more than eighteen stone — used to breakfast on competition days on two pounds of steak along with six raw eggs still in their shells! He was also well fed on success, winning the shot at the 1904 and 1908 Olympics and taking the silver in 1912 in Stockholm where he was the gold medallist in the two-handed shot. He was also second in the discus and third in the hammer in the 1904 Games in St Louis. Rose volunteered to act as anchorman for the United States tug-of-war team in the 1908 London Olympics at the White City. He and his team-mates angrily pulled out of the competition after a defeat against a British squad who, they claimed, were wearing illegal heavy boots.

HEIDE ROSENDAHL
West Germany (1947)
The daughter of a former German discus champion, Heide Rosendahl was the darling of West German athletics for six years during which she proved herself one of the world's finest all-round sportswomen but — until the 1972 Munich Games — missing out on the major titles. She went to the 1968 Olympics in Mexico as a favourite for the long jump and pentathlon but a stomach upset and then a muscle injury prevented her making any sort of impact. Four years later in front of her adoring fans in Munich, Heide won the long jump with a leap of 22ft 3in (6.78m), just eight centimetres short of the world record she had set in 1970. She was narrowly beaten into second place by the inspired Mary Peters in a memorable pentathlon and then overhauled East Germany's Renate Stecher on the anchor leg of the sprint relay to bring West Germany home in first place in a world-record-equalling 42.81 sec.

NORMAN ROSS
United States (1896-1953)
A front-line war hero in the First World War, Norman Ross was acclaimed in the immediate post-war years as a hero of the swimming pool. He won the 400 and 1500 metres freestyle titles in the 1920 Olympics and helped the United States team win the 4 x 200 metres relay gold medal. Married to a Hawaiian princess, Chicago-born Ross was a large man standing 6ft 2in and weighing more than fifteen stone. He had a tremendously strong arm-pull and a powerful scis

sors kick that enabled him to drive through the water at high speeds that he could sustain for lengths on end. His thirteen world records for all the recognized freestyle distances from 200 metres to 880 yards and his eighteen US national titles provide positive evidence of his domination in the pool. When he retired he became a popular radio presenter of classical music programmes.

WILMA RUDOLPH
United States (1940)

The twentieth of a family of twenty-two children, Wilma Rudolph was one of the most remarkable women ever to set foot on a running track. An illness when she was a baby robbed her of the use of her left leg and she could only walk with the aid of a steel brace until she was twelve. She was encouraged to take up sports to help build up the wasted muscle in her leg and she became an outstanding high school basketball player in her native Tennessee. Athletics coach Ed Temple spotted the speed with which she

Wilma Rudolph: the 'Tennessee Tigress'

moved around the court and took her under his wing. At the end of her first season she won a place in the US Olympic squad for the 1956 Games in Melbourne, and at just sixteen helped the sprint relay squad collect a bronze medal. By the time of the Rome Games four years later she had blossomed into a world-beater. With a mixture of controlled power and graceful elegance, the beautiful, long-limbed 'Tennessee Tigress' streaked to a hat-trick of gold medals in the 100 metres, 200 metres and the sprint relay. She equalled the world record of 11.3 sec for l00 metres in the heats and then scorched to victory in the final in a breath-taking 11.0 sec which didn't make the record books because of a following wind. Wilma lowered the record to 11.2 sec in 1961 before retiring from a sport she had lit up with her talent and her dazzling smile.

PADDY RYAN
United States (1882-1964)

Paddy Ryan was born and died in County Limerick but it was in the United States that he became a world-renowned hammer-thrower. A 6ft 4in, twenty-stone colossus, Ryan first came to prominence when as a near novice he beat renowned hammer expert Tom Kiely in the 1902 Irish championships. His progress was slow after this initial success and it was not until he emigrated to the United States eight years later that he started to live up to his early promise. He won eight American championships in nine years and at the age of thirty-seven won the Olympic gold medal in the 1920 Antwerp Games. Ryan, who also took the silver medal in the 56 lb weight throw, set a world record of 189ft 6in in 1913 which lasted for twenty-five years and survived as an American record until 1953. Legends grew up around Ryan, a genial giant who was popular with all his team-mates and opponents. It was claimed that he was flying high on alcohol when he made his Olympic title-winning throw, an allegation that he always laughed off. Ryan, one of the school of Irish-American 'whales'(so called because of their huge bulk) who dominated the he-man throwing events in the first quarter of the century, followed countrymen John Flanagan and Matt McGrath as Olympic champion. They were born within twenty miles of each other in Ireland and all represented the United States in the Olympics.

VIKTOR SANEYEV
USSR (1945)

No athletics event puts as much stress and strain on an athlete's legs as the triple jump, which makes Victor Saneyev's achievement of three successive Olympic gold medals all the more astonishing. He started out as a high-jumper until a knee injury forced a change of direction and he developed into a world-class long-jumper and triple jumper. Saneyev won his first Olympic title in the thin air of Mexico in 1968 in a memorable contest during which three competitors broke the world record five times between them. He overcame recurring injury problems to retain the title in 1972 and 1976 and made a valiant attempt for a fourth gold medal in Moscow in 1980 when he finished second with an effort of 17.24 metres, his best performance for four years, and at the advanced age of thirty-five.

DON SCHOLLANDER
United States (1946)
Don Schollander made history in the pool at the 1964 Tokyo Olympics when he became the first swimmer to win four gold medals at one Games. He took the 100 metres freestyle sprint title by a touch from Scottish hero Bobby McGregor and captured the 400 metres crown in a world record 4 min 12.2 sec. Schollander then anchored the United States relay teams to two titles, both won in world record times. A great exponent of the front crawl technique, he added a fifth gold medal in the 200 metres freestyle relay in Mexico in 1968 and collected a silver behind powerful Australian Mike Wenden in the 200 metres freestyle. Schollander — who later graduated from

Yale as a lawyer — established himself as an outstanding coach after a career in which he set thirteen world records in individual events and shared in eight relay world records. He swam for the Santa Clara Club in California and turned the 200 metres freestyle into *his* event, lowering the world record nine times and becoming the first man to break the two-minute barrier. He brought the record down to 1 min 54.3 sec before his retirement.

BORIS SHAKHLIN
USSR (1932)
There have been more exciting and inventive gymnasts than Boris Shakhlin but rarely any to match his technique and efficiency. He amassed nineteen gold, ten silver and four bronze medals in Olympic, world and European championships during a twelve-year international career that established him as one of the great masters of the gymnasium. At 5ft 7½ in and 11 stone, he was physically bigger than most of his rivals but he lacked nothing in mobility, while his powerful forearms made him particularly successful on the pommelled horse and horizontal bars. He was a major force at the 1956, 1960 and 1964 Olympics, with his peak performance coming in the 1960 Rome Games when he held off a strong challenge from the all-conquering Japanese to win the combined exercises title.

Don Schollander: the king of the crawl

FRANK SHORTER
United States (1947)

Born in Munich to American parents, Frank Shorter returned to the city of his birth to win the 1972 Olympic marathon. It was a triumph that did more than anything else to trigger the jogging and long-distance running explosion in the United States where thousands of people were literally brought to their feet by Shorter's success. Lancashire-born Derek Clayton, running for Australia, set the sort of blistering pace that had made him the fastest marathon runner in history but he could not shake off the determined American. Clayton became a victim of his own suicidal tempo and as he slipped back to ninth place Shorter pushed to the front and went on to win in 2 hr 12 min 19.8 sec. During the first week of the Munich Games Shorter had twice lowered the American 10,000 metres record, finishing fifth in the final in 27 min 51.4 sec. Four times a winner of the classic Fukuoka marathon in Japan, Shorter went to Montreal for the 1976 Olympics favourite to retain his title. But having to run in a US Olympic trial just five weeks before the Games took the edge off Shorter's form and he was forced into second place by the fast-finishing East German Waldemar Cierpinski.

ADHEMAR FERREIRA da SILVA
Brazil (1927)

This silky-smooth triple-jumper from São Paulo was the first Brazilian athlete to win an Olympic gold medal and the first South American champion in the field events. Da Silva gave little indication of the glory that was to come when he finished eleventh in the 1948 Olympics in London but revealed his full power two years later when he set the first of his five world records. Coached by German jumping expert Dietrich Gerner, he won the 1952 Olympic title in impressive style — equalling or bettering his world record with four of his six leaps. He showed his great competitive qualities in the 1956 Melbourne Games when he came from behind to retain his title. He closed his distinguished Olympic career at the age of thirty-three in Rome in 1960 when he finished fourteenth, his first defeat in a major championship for nine years.

TOMMIE SMITH
United States (1944)

There were two stunning demonstrations of 'Black power' from Tommie Smith during the 1968 Olympics in Mexico City. The first came in the 200 metres final when, despite the handicap of a groin muscle injury, he surged to victory in the 200 metres final in a world record 19.83 sec which would have been even quicker had he not thrown his arms up in triumph two metres before the tape. The second show of 'Black power' came on the victory rostrum when he and silver medallist John Carlos each raised a gloved hand in a clenched fist salute and in the other hand flourished a black 'Puma' track shoe. The clenched fist represented Black power and unity and the shoe was a protest against commercialism. Both Smith and Carlos, who bowed their heads during the playing of the American national anthem, were immediately expelled by the US Olympic Committee but they had made their point. 'If I do something good then I am an American,' Smith explained. 'If I do something bad I'm a Negro.'

This controversial incident could not overshadow the fact that Smith was as talented a sprinter as there has ever been. He could maintain phenomenal speed for distances up to 400 metres and set world records for 200 metres and 220 yards on a straight and a curved course, at 400 metres and 440 yards and missed the 100 metres record by just 0.1 sec. The 6ft 3in, Texas-born San Jose College student was a worthy successor to Henry Carr, another power-propelled Black sprinter who won the 200 metres gold medal in the 1964 Olympics. Smith, a 26-foot long-jumper, joined the professional circuit after the Olympics, and is now a respected coach.

PETER SNELL
New Zealand (1938)

The athletics world had little knowledge of Peter Snell when he exploded on the scene as a shock winner of the Olympic 800 metres final in the 1960 Rome Olympics, beating Belgian world record holder Roger Moens by a stride in 1 min 46.3 sec. It was an improvement of nearly three seconds on his pre-Games best performance set in the days when he was more interested in lawn tennis than running. Over the next four years 'the man in black' from Opunake became recognized as one of the most famous and respected middle-distance runners of all time and proved well fitted to carry on the torch lit by his countryman Jack Lovelock in the 1936 Olympics. Following a punishing training programme set by his coach, Arthur Lydiard, powerfully built Snell gained stamina to go with his strength and speed and set world records at 800 metres, 880 yards, 1000 metres and the mile. He ran eleven sub-four minute miles and was never beaten when it really mattered.

Snell had to live in the shadow of the recently retired Herb Elliott but became a superstar in his own right in the 1964 Olympics in Tokyo when he won the 800 metres and 1500 metres, virtually toying with top-flight opposition in both finals before pulverizing them with a blistering finishing spurt. Lydiard, a former distance-running champion, shaped Snell into an all-purposes runner. He ducked under 48 seconds in a 440 yards race and clocked 2 hours 41 min 11 sec over the marathon course. Snell retired in 1965 after two defeats by up-and-coming American teenager Jim Ryun convinced him that he was past his golden peak.

Peter Snell: toyed with the opposition

Mark Spitz: a medal blitz in Munich

LEON (1953) and MIKE (1956) SPINKS
United States

The Spinks brothers, from St Louis, Missouri, were prominent members of the extremely successful United States team in the 1976 Montreal Olympics. Leon captured the light-heavyweight championship and Mike — two inches taller, but nearly a stone lighter — won the middleweight gold medal. Both then went on to win world titles as professionals. Ex-marine Leon scored a sensational points victory over Muhammad Ali to take the world heavyweight crown in only his eighth paid contest, but was dethroned by the amazing Ali in a return fight. Not since 1956 Olympic heavyweight champion Pete Rademacher fought and lost to Floyd Patterson for the world title in his debut had such an inexperienced boxer as Spinks challenged for professional boxing's peak prize. His younger brother Mike became WBA light-heavyweight champion in his seventeenth professional contest. They were the two eldest of seven children raised in a rundown area of St Louis and they took up boxing to keep out of trouble on the tough neighbourhood streets. Their father left home when they were in their early teens and they were raised by their Bible-teaching mother.

MARK SPITZ
United States (1950)

Mark Spitz knew he had to achieve something special in the swimming-pool at the 1972 Munich Olympics to wipe out the memory of his comparative failure in the 1968 Games when his two relay gold medals did

not come close to what he had been verbally promising to achieve. He provided action to go with his words in Munich, winning a record seven gold medals. Spitz won the 100 and 200 metres freestyle; the 100 and 200 metres butterfly; and he helped the United States teams win the three sprint relays. The 'Spitz blitz' was even more remarkable in that a world record was set every time he touched home for gold. A dental student, he was coached at the Arden Hills Club, California, by Sherman Chavoor. He was cleared by the International Olympic Committee of accusations of commercialism during the 1972 Games but later cashed in on his fame with advertising and endorsement contracts said to be worth more than a million dollars. Spitz — who it was claimed had to contend with feelings of anti-Semitism early in his career — broke or equalled a total of thirty-two world records. While he was supreme over the sprints, he was also strong at distance events, as he proved when coming within four-tenths of a second of the 1500 metres freestyle world record in 1966 when aged sixteen.

TEOFILO STEVENSON
Cuba (1951)
Nicknamed 'Castro's Hit Man', there is little doubt that Teofilo Stevenson would have earned a fortune in the professional ring had he been allowed to box for pay. He is the only boxer to have won three successive Olympic heavyweight titles and was reputed to have turned down millions of dollars to fight Muhammad Ali for the world professional championship. Coached by a Russian, this 6ft 3in, 15-stone son of a Jamaican father and a Cuban mother had Ali-like looks and ringcraft but was unquestionably a harder puncher than the man with whom he was always being compared. The way he dispatched American champions Duane Bobick (second round) and John Tate (first round) in the 1972 and 1976 Games respectively provided positive proof that he was as devastating a puncher as has ever been seen in the amateur ring. Stevenson, who studied mechanical engineering, was anything but mechanical in the ring. He boxed with intelligence, making the openings for his thunderous right hand punches with a probing left jab. The giant Cuban looked past his peak at the 1980 Moscow Olympics but was still a class above any of the other boxers in the heavyweight division. He comfortably completed his hat-trick, equalling the three-title record set by the Hungarian middleweight Laszlo Papp. He was also world amateur heavyweight champion in 1974 and 1978.

SHIRLEY STRICKLAND
Australia (1925)
The daughter of a noted professional sprinter and hurdler, Shirley Strickland followed in her father's

Teofilo Stevenson: 'Castro's Hit Man'

footsteps and became one of the most successful women athletes in Olympic history. Shirley, a tall, lithe blonde who used to chase kangaroos on the farm in Guilford, Western Australia, where she was born, was overshadowed by the 'Flying Dutchwoman' Fanny Blankers-Koen when she made her Olympics debut in London in 1948 after graduating from university. But her rich potential was there for all to see as she collected bronze medals in the 100 metres and 80 metres hurdles, finished fourth in the 200 metres and helped the Australian sprint relay team take the silver medal. Four years later in Helsinki (and by then Mrs De la Hunty) she set a new world record of 10.9 sec when winning the gold medal in the 80 metres hurdles, came third in the 100 metres and ran a storming relay leg to set Australia up with a victory chance that was ruined by a disastrous last-leg baton pass.

When she became a mother at the age of twenty-eight, most people assumed her international athletics career was over. But 'Queen of the Track' Shirley had her best days ahead of her. A year later in

Warsaw she set a new world record of 11.3 sec for 100 metres and reached a peak the following year in front of her adoring fans in the 1956 Melbourne Olympics when she won the 80 metres hurdles and helped the Australian sprint relay squad to victory in a new world record. On her retirement from international competition Shirley continued to serve athletics in an official capacity and as a coach who occasionally competed with and beat her pupils.

OSCAR (1847-1927) and ALFRED (1879-1931) SWAHN
Sweden

Oscar and Alfred Swahn literally shot to Olympic fame and together hold the record for a family collection of medals. The remarkable Oscar was a trigger-happy rifleman who competed in international events for a golden stretch of sixty years. At seventy-two he took part in the 1920 Antwerp Games to become the oldest competitor in Olympic history. Four years later he again won Olympic selection but ill-health forced his withdrawal at the last minute. Deadeye Oscar was a champion marksman in the 1908, 1912 and 1920 Games and won three gold medals, one silver and two bronze, all of them in the running deer single and double shot competitions. His son Alfred inherited his skill and deadly accuracy and was a crack shot while still a schoolboy. He competed in four Olympics, the first three in the same team as his father and then again in 1924 when he took his personal medals haul to three golds, one silver and one bronze.

IRENA SZEWINSKA
Poland (1946)

An immortal of women's athletics, Irena Szewinska was a major power in both track and field for more than sixteen years. She revealed her astonishing range of talent when as eighteen-year-old Miss Kirszenstein she finished second in both the long-jump and 200 metres in the 1964 Tokyo Olympics and then picked up a gold medal as a member of Poland's sprint relay team. Four years later in Mexico she won the 200 metres in a world record 22.5 sec and was a bronze medallist in the 100 metres. Another medal seemed hers for the taking in the sprint relay but in her eagerness to clinch a place in the final she dropped the baton. The modest and likeable Irena was extremely distressed, not for herself but for her team-mates whom she felt she had let down. Marriage and the birth of a son interrupted her training schedule before the 1972 Munich Games but she still managed a bronze medal in the 200 metres.

Irena, born in Leningrad but brought up in Poland, had stepped up to 400 metres by the time of the 1976 Montreal Olympics and brought a new dimension to the event when she became the first woman to break the 50 sec barrier. She lowered her own world record to 49.28 sec on her way to victory in the Montreal final by a margin of ten metres. The 'First Lady' of athletics won ten medals in European championships and wound down her glorious career with an appearance in the Moscow Olympics at the age of thirty-four when a leg injury prevented her reaching the 400 metres final in defence of her crown.

Irena Szewinska: astonishing range of talent

JOZEF SZMIDT
Poland (1935)

He will always be remembered as the man who first surpassed the 55 feet and 17 metre targets in the triple jump, an event in which he was Olympic champion in 1960 and 1964 and European gold medallist in 1958 and 1962. Szmidt and his elder brother, Edward, were two of Poland's leading sprinters and Jozef was also a near-26ft long-jumper. Despite a succession of leg and ankle injuries, Jozef kept competing at top international level until the age of thirty-seven and produced the longest triple jump of his Olympic career (16.89m) in the 1968 Games when he finished seventh.

HENRY TAYLOR
Great Britain (1885-1951)

Henry Taylor progressed from swimming in the Lancashire shipping canals to making a golden splash in the Olympic pool. An orphan from Chadderton, near Oldham, he was raised by an elder brother who encouraged him to take up swimming as a pastime. He went on to win fifteen English championships, starting with the 440 yards 'salt water' title at the turn of the century and finishing with the five miles river Thames championship in 1920 at the age of thirty-five. Taylor's greatest triumphs came in the 1908 London Olympics when, competing in the 100 metre pool erected on the inner field at the White City athletics stadium, he won the 400 and 1500 metre finals in world record times and anchored the British team to victory in the 4 x 200 metres relay. Two years earlier he had competed in the 1906 'Interim Olympics' in Athens and finished first in the one mile freestyle and second in the 400 metres freestyle. He collected relay bronze medals in the 1912 and 1920 Olympics before giving up his job in a Lancashire mill to become a publican. The business venture was a flop, and having sold many of his trophies to pay off debts, he became a pool attendant at the Chadderton baths where he had perfected his technique as a young swimmer.

DAVID THEILE
Australia (1938)

The son of a Queensland doctor, David Theile (pronounced 'Tyler') shared his time between studies to become a surgeon and training as a backstroke swimmer. The fact that he got both his medical degree and gold medals in the 100 metres backstroke at the 1956 and 1960 Olympics proves that his time-sharing worked to perfection. He beat his great Australian rival John Monckton into second place by three clear seconds when breaking the world record in the 1956 final, the greatest victory margin recorded in an Olympic swimming sprint event. Theile had just 0.2 sec to spare over American Frank McKinney in the 1960 Games in Rome where he also took a silver medal in the medley relay.

DON THOMPSON
Great Britain (1933)

Olympic heroes have rarely come more determined or plucky than Don Thompson, Britain's lone athletics gold medallist in the 1960 Games. He had collapsed with exhaustion in the closing stages of the 50 kilometres walk in the 1956 Olympics and had vowed to make proper preparations for the Rome Games four years later. He got himself acclimatized for the sultry heat of Italy by turning the bathroom at his home into a steam room where he used to follow a series of explosive exercises while wearing a track-suit in temperatures of around 100 degrees Fahrenheit. The small, bespectacled insurance clerk — dubbed 'Little Mouse' by the Press — was rewarded for his thoroughness with an inspiring victory in an Olympic record 4 hr 25 min 30 sec after he had fought off a strong challenge from 1948 champion John Ljunggren, a 41-year-old Swede. Thompson had started his athletics career as a long-distance runner but switched to walking after an injury had handicapped his running. He won the 52-mile London to Brighton walk for eight successive years and was British national 50 kilometre champion six times in a row. Despite an improvement of nearly three minutes on his winning time in Rome, Thompson could only finish tenth when defending his Olympic title in Tokyo in 1964.

JIM THORPE
United States (1888-1953)

Jim Thorpe, the greatest all-round athlete of the first half of the century, suffered the ignominy of being ordered to return the two gold medals he won in the pentathlon and decathlon at the 1912 Olympics in Stockholm. 'Sir,' the King of Sweden had told Thorpe when introduced to him at the victory ceremony, 'you are the most wonderful athlete in the world.' Legend has it that Thorpe replied, 'Thanks, King.' Six months after this pleasant exchange, Thorpe was disqualified and his name removed from the official Olympic record books because it was discovered that he had received $60 expenses for playing baseball soon after leaving school. When confronted with the evidence Thorpe did not try to deny it but said simply: 'I had no idea accepting expenses infringed my amateur status. I didn't play for the money. I played because I like baseball.' The IOC showed a lack of compassion and stripped Thorpe of his honours and it wasn't until more than seventy years later that a campaign to reinstate him as the rightful dual champion was successful and the name Jim Thorpe was rewritten into the record books.

Thorpe was a full-blooded Indian whose mother was from the Potawatome tribe and his father from the Sac and Fox tribe. His tribal name was Wa-Tho-Huck, meaning Bright Path. Born in Shawnee, Oklahoma, he went to an Indian school in Carlisle, Pennsylvania, and once represented the athletics

Jim Thorpe: reinstated as a dual champion

Los Angeles. An Irishman who was born in Ceylon, Tisdall didn't blossom as an athlete until arriving at Cambridge University where 1928 Olympic champion Lord Burghley had perfected his hurdling technique. He revealed fine all-round talent and set his mind on going to Los Angeles as a decathlete but a victory over Lord Burghley in a 220 yards hurdles race early in Olympic year persuaded him to try his luck at the longer event. Tisdall wrote to the Irish selectors asking to be considered for the decathlon and the 400 metres hurdles and, somewhat reluctantly, they picked him after he had run an unimpressive time trial. He and his wife moved to a converted railway carriage in an orchard in Sussex three months before the Games so that he could concentrate on getting himself fully fit with daily runs over the rolling Sussex Downs.

Nobody, including Tisdall himself, gave him a chance of winning the gold medal or even of reaching the Olympic final in which Lord Burghley, Italian ace Luigi Facelli and crack Americans Glenn Hardin and Morgan Taylor were all considered capable of taking the title. But he began to emerge as a dark horse after winning his heat in 54.8 sec and then the semi-final in an Olympic record-equalling 52.8 sec — a victory that he celebrated with several glasses of champagne despite the final scheduled for the next day. Tisdall set off in the fifth (and last) 400 metres hurdles race of his life like a man with a gun at his back. He led all the way from the first hurdle and went through the tape in 51.7 sec, which would have been a world record had he not knocked over the final barrier. Glenn Hardin was credited with a new world record as he crossed the line in second place in 51.9 sec. Just ten minutes later the champagne was flowing again as Ireland's Dr Pat O'Callaghan retained the hammer title with his final throw. It was a great day for the hundreds of Irish-Americans in the Olympic Stadium. Tisdall raised their hopes of further glory when he led at the end of the first day of the decathlon but slipped away to a final eighth place.

team in an inter-schools match on his own. Thorpe competed in eight events and won them all. He was in sensational form in the Stockholm Olympics, winning four of the five pentathlon events and taking the decathlon title with a lead of more than seven hundred points over his nearest rival. A man of incredible energy, he also finished fourth in the individual high jump and seventh in the long jump. He became a formidable force in American football after he had been barred from amateur athletics and was voted the athlete of the half-century in 1950.

BOB TISDALL
Ireland (1907)
Bob Tisdall, shock winner of the 400 metres hurdles in the 1932 Olympics, had run only two competitive races in the 'man killer' event prior to the Games in

EDDIE TOLAN
United States (1908-1967)
Eddie Tolan, nicknamed 'The Midnight Express', was the first of a long line of black American Olympic sprint champions. He had already established himself in the record books as the first man to clock 9.5 sec for 100 yards and proved this was no one-off performance by winning both the 100 and 200 metres in the 1932 Los Angeles Olympics. His victory in the 100 metres in a world record equalling 10.3 sec was achieved by the narrowest margin in the history of the Olympics. Close study of the official film of the Games showed him to be just one inch ahead of fellow black American Ralph Metcalfe who had beaten him into second place in both sprints in the US championships the previous month. Tolan, a stocky, bespectacled powerhouse of a runner with tre-

mendously fast leg speed, left no room for doubt in the 200 metres final, winning by two metres in a new Olympic record 21.2 sec.

BILL TOOMEY
United States (1939)
Big Bill Toomey was beaten in only three out of twenty-two decathlons between 1966 and 1969, retiring after setting a world record in his final competition. He was so keen to collect as much knowledge as possible about his speciality event that he paid his own fare to Tokyo in 1964 to watch the decathlon after failing to qualify for the US team. His determination and dedication paid off when he won the Pan American title in 1967 and then the 1968 Olympic crown in Mexico where the high altitude cost him the chance of a world record after he had set a blistering pace in the early events. He overcame an enormous handicap to prove himself the world's greatest all-round athlete. An accident when he was a child had left him with a semi-paralysed right hand which restricted his output in the three throwing events and the pole vault. Bill, who married Britain's athletics golden girl Mary Rand, is now a business executive in California.

FORREST TOWNS
United States (1914)
Forrest Towns took the art of high hurdling into new territory when he became the first man to break the 14 seconds barrier in August 1936. He lowered the world's best for 110 metres hurdles by an incredible 0.4 sec to 13.7 sec during a pre-Olympic run in Oslo. The athletics world (including Towns!) was sceptical about the time and the IAAF were convinced a mistake had been made. It was only after two years and careful study of film of the race that they at last ratified it as a record. The towering Towns, a 6ft 2in inter-collegiate champion, had meantime added the Olympic crown to his prize list with a convincing victory over Britain's Don Finlay in 14.2 sec.

PIERRE TRENTIN
France (1944)
Built like an ox, Pierre Trentin was a powerful force in world amateur track cycle racing in the 1960s. His greatest performances came in the Mexico Olympics in 1968 when he drove himself to the edge of exhaustion to take the gold medal in the 1000 metres time trial. He collapsed at the end of his winning, world-record-breaking ride and had to be carried to the dressing-rooms. There was concern about his health but he made a rapid recovery to share another gold medal in the tandem sprint with his close friend and perpetual rival Daniel Morelon. He also collected a bronze medal in the individual sprint.

YOSHIYUKI TSURUTA
Japan (1903)
This power-propelled breaststroke specialist led Japan's domination of the Olympic swimming pool between the wars. He became the only swimmer to score a double victory in Olympic breaststroke events when he retained his 200 metres title in the Los Angeles Games in 1932. Tsuruta had smashed the Olympic record by a stunning 7.8 sec in 1928 when winning the gold medal in 2 min 48.8 sec and the following year lowered the world record to 2 min 45 sec in a 25-metre pool in Kyoto. In Los Angeles he knocked another 3.4 sec off his Olympic record as the all-conquering Japanese collected eleven out of a possible sixteen swimming gold medals.

WYOMIA TYUS
United States (1945)
Wyomia Tyus laid a strong claim for consideration as one of the greatest women sprinters of all time when she became the first athlete, male or female, to win an Olympic sprint title twice. From the same Tennessee State University team that produced 1960 champion Wilma Rudolph, Wyomia succeeded Wilma as 100 metres gold medallist in the 1964 Tokyo Games and equalled her 11.2 sec world record in a heat. Four years later, the Tennessee Tigerbelle scorched over a rain-soaked track in the high altitude of Mexico City to retain her title in a world record 11.00 sec dead. Georgia-born Wyomia added a sprint relay gold to the silver she had picked up in Tokyo when, despite casual and almost catastrophic baton-changing, she anchored the United States team to victory in a world record 42.8 sec.

LASSE VIREN
Finland (1949)
For Lasse Viren — the man who pumped the pride back into Finnish middle-distance running — the Olympics were everything. He motivated himself solely for Olympic glory and never lost sleep over what, by his skyscraping standards, were occasional mediocre performances between the Games. Viren, then a rather shy, obscure village policeman, exploded into the world spotlight when he won both the 5000 and 10,000 metres in the 1972 Olympics in Munich. It was a golden double achieved before by only three track giants — his countryman Hannes Kolehmainen, galloping Czech Emil Zatopek and Russian iron man Vladimir Kuts. He showed he had tremendous competitive qualities to go with his talent when he recovered from a fall in the 10,000 metres final to win in a world record 27 min 38.4 sec, covering the last 800 metres in a mind-blowing 1 min 56.2 sec. Viren had started that memorable 1972 season with a world record over two miles and finished it by lowering the 5000 metres world record to 13 min 16.4 sec.

Lasse Viren: winning the 5000 metres in Montreal

The latest of the 'Flying Finns' went to Montreal to defend his titles in 1976 with a lot of people ready to write him off. He had displayed indifferent form and had been into hospital for a hamstring operation and again for what was reported to be nasal surgery. But Viren had got himself into peak condition for the races that really mattered and became the first man in history to retain both the 5000 and 10,000 championships — a magnificent achievement that put him right up on the popularity pedestal with Kohlemainen and Paavo Nurmi, those two Olympic immortals in whose shadow all Finns have to run. Viren then tried to equal Zatopek's triple triumph of 1952 by making a bid for the marathon gold medal the day after his victory in the 5000 metres. He ran a gallant race and was always in touch with the leaders but his exhausting efforts of the previous eight days finally caught up with him and he proved he was human by dropping back to fifth place. After another four years of fairly mediocre performances, Viren returned to the Olympic stage in Moscow but this time there were to be no miracles. He briefly took the lead with three laps to go in the 10,000 metres, only to be outkicked by four faster finishers in a last hectic rush for medal positions. The spark had gone out of his

running but he had lit an Olympic flame with his earlier achievements that will never be extinguished. Kolehmainen. Nurmi. Viren. You can mention them in the same breath.

JOHN WALKER
New Zealand (1952)
John Walker has been a master miler for more than a decade and carries on gloriously the tradition set by his countrymen Jack Lovelock and Peter Snell who — like Walker — lowered the world mile record and then struck gold in the Olympic 1500 metres final. For a man who has run close to a hundred sub-four minute miles, Walker hardly seems an appropriate name! He will always have a place in the record books as the first miler to break 3 min 50 sec, a sensational performance in Gothenburg in 1975 when he produced a last lap of 56.4 sec to finish in 3 min 49.4 sec — exactly ten seconds faster than Roger Bannister's first four-minute mile twenty-one years earlier.

The son of a champion cyclist and all-round sportsman, Walker first emerged as a world star when he chased Tanzanian Filbert Bayi all the way to the line in a classic Commonwealth Games 1500 metres final in 1974. Both men finished inside Jim Ryun's world record and Walker avenged his narrow defeat by Bayi in Helsinki later in the year. Motivated

by coach Arch Jelley, the New Zealander got himself into peak condition for a scheduled 'decider' with Bayi in the 1976 Montreal Olympics. He proved he was in great shape by smashing Michel Jazy's world 2000 metres record during his build-up to the Games but then had to suffer an anticlimax when the African boycott robbed him of Bayi's challenge. Walker ran well within himself in the 1500 metres final, pouring all his considerable energy and speed into a 52.7 sec last lap for a narrow yet convincing victory in a relatively slow 3 min 39.2 sec. A succession of injuries and major surgery that would have pushed many athletes into retirement has anchored Walker's progress but he remains one of the world's top ten milers and his great competitive spirit will make him a formidable opponent in Los Angeles.

JOHNNY WEISSMULLER
United States (1904-1984)
Both in and out of the water, Johnny Weissmuller was a legendary figure. He won three gold medals in the 1924 Olympics in Paris and two more in Amsterdam four years later and he still has a lot of support in debates as to who has been the swimmer of the century. Standing 6ft 3in and superbly sculptured, he became even more famous at the end of his amateur career when he landed the plum Hollywood role of the screen's first talking Tarzan. No stuntman was needed for the daring dives and jet-propelled swims in crocodile-infested waters! His honours haul in the swimming pool speaks for itself: fifty-two US titles, twenty-eight ratified freestyle world records from 100 yards to 880 yards and also for the 150 yards backstroke. He perfected the front crawl technique at the Illinois Athletic Club under the expert eye of coach Bill Bachrach and began breaking world records at the age of seventeen.

Weissmuller was the first man to break the 60 seconds barrier in the 100 metres in 1922 and his world record of 51 sec for 100 yards in 1927 went unbeaten for seventeen years. He also opened new horizons at 440 yards when he became the first swimmer to beat five minutes in 1923. In the 1924 Olympics, he not only won the 100 and 400 metres and helped the US relay team to first place but also found the energy to take part in the water polo matches and was rewarded with a bronze medal. He retained the 100 metres title in 1928 and completed his then record gold medal collection in the 4 x 200 metres relay. Weissmuller turned professional in 1929 and earned a fortune with his acting and exhibition swimming. At the age of thirty-six he achieved a personal best 48.5 sec for 100 yards. Always a popular personality, he struggled to hang on to his vast fortune because of crippling alimony he had to pay to

Johnny Weissmuller: a star in and out of the water

five ex-wives. Sadly, he died right at the start of this Olympic year, but his name will live on in Olympic and Hollywood history.

ALLAN WELLS
Great Britain (1952)
They don't come gutsier or more competitive than Allan Wells, who has proved himself one of the outstanding white sprinters of all time. The 'Flying

Opposite
John Walker: carrying on a tradition

Scot' from Edinburgh became at twenty-eight the oldest man ever to win an Olympic 100 metres sprint title when he beat Cuban Silvio Leonard by the width of a running vest in 10.25 sec. It was the first British victory in this event since Harold Abrahams triumphed in Paris in 1924 and the first Scottish success in any track and field event since Eric Liddell's 400 metres win at the same Paris Games. There were comments from across the Atlantic that Wells would never have won if the Americans had not boycotted the Games but that is all hypothetical. He won when and where it mattered and nobody can ever take his Olympic medal away from him. The muscular, 13-stone Scot very nearly pulled off a double in the 200 metres when only a blistering finish by his old Italian rival Pietro Mennea prevented him collecting two gold medals.

Wells has literally made rapid strides since starting his athletics career as a long-jumper and triple jumper who volunteered to rake the pit at the 1970 Commonwealth Games in Edinburgh so that he could study the technique of his idol Lynn Davies. Motivated by his wife Margot (herself a British international sprinter), Wells had his early successes without use of starting blocks until they became compulsory at the Moscow Olympics. His training technique was based on old, well-proven Scottish traditions that included work-outs on a boxing punchball to help speed his reflexes and develop his already impressive upper body. He won a gold in the 200 metres and a silver in the 100 in the 1978 Commonwealth championships and was a gold medallist in both events four years later, sharing the 200 metres title after a dead-heat with Mike McFarlane. His great fighting qualities were again revealed in the 1983 world championships in Helsinki when, after his training programme had been disrupted by injuries, he managed to finish fourth in the 100 metres final behind three outstanding black American sprinters led by the incomparable Carl Lewis. He will be thirty-four by the time of the LA Olympics but has the sort of tough mental attitude that will make him a force still to be reckoned with.

MIKE WENDEN
Australia (1949)
Mike Wenden switched from football to swimming literally by accident after breaking a leg as a thirteen-year-old schoolboy in Liverpool, New South Wales. He was encouraged to swim as a therapeutic exercise and within three years had established himself as one of the world's most powerful sprint swimmers. Wenden won three gold medals at the 1966 Commonwealth Games and two years later scored a superb double-gold victory over the crack Americans in the Olympic pool in Mexico. He prepared for the 1968 Games by swimming up to 15,000 metres a day in training under the demanding supervision of his coach Vic Arneil who introduced a series of isometric

exercises to shape and strengthen his frame. Using an unorthodox yet effective 'windmill' stroke, he hurtled to first place in the 100 metres freestyle in a world record 52.2 sec and added the 200 metres title in an Olympic record 1 min 52.2 sec, defeating the great Don Schollander on the way. He had to swim in the wake of Mark Spitz in the 1972 Munich Games — finishing fifth and fourth in his speciality sprint events — but remained one of the world's top competitors for another two years.

MAL WHITFIELD
United States (1924)
This tall, silky-smooth stylist was the finest two-lap runner in the world during the immediate post-war years and won gold medals in the 800 metres at the 1948 and 1952 Olympics with what were identical performances. He held off the strong challenge of long-striding Jamaican Arthur Wint to win the title at Wembley in 1948 in 1 min 49.2 sec. Four years later in Helsinki Whitfield and Wint were locked together in a carbon-copy contest and — as in 1948 — it was the Texas-born American who got to the tape first, while again the clock stopped at 1 min 49.2 sec. He lost only three of sixty-nine two-lap races in a six-year span between 1948 and 1954 and also had success in a whole range of other events including a 10.7 sec 100 metres and a mile in 4 min 12.6 sec.

Whitfield went for the 400-800 double at both the 1948 and 1952 Games, finishing third in the one-lap event in London and sixth in Helsinki. He helped the United States 4 x 400 metres squad take the gold in 1948 and a silver four years later. The European circuit brought out the best in him. He set a world record of 1 min 48.6 for 880 yards in Finland in July, 1953, and the next month in Sweden clocked a world record of 2 min 20.8 sec for 1000 metres, following this just an hour later with an American record 46.2 sec for 440 yards. He closed his distinguished career in 1956 after just failing to qualify for the Melbourne Games. Twenty years later he was a fascinated spectator at the Montreal Olympics when Alberto Juantorena completed the 400-800 double that had eluded him. As 'White Lightning' Juantorena crossed the finishing line in the 800 metres in a world record 1 min 43.5 sec, Whitfield — the 'Mr Smooth' of athletics — shook his head and said: 'The event has changed out of sight since my day. This man Juantorena has turned it into a sprint!'

HAROLD WHITLOCK
Great Britain (1903)
To Harold Whitlock, walking was a way of life. He retained the Olympic 50 kilometres walk title for Britain in 1936 four years after Tommy Green had won it in the 1932 Los Angeles Games. It was the high spot of an international career that continued until he was forty-eight. He made his final appear

ance in a British vest at the 1952 Olympics when he finished a gallant eleventh, with his younger brother, Rex, coming in fourth. Harold continued to serve the sport he loved as Britain's national walking coach and his son, Terry, was one of his most enthusiastic pupils. He was six times British 50 kilometres champion in the seven years immediately before the Second World War and in 1935 set a world record for the 30 mile track walk when he circled the White City track 200 times in 4 hr 29 min 31.8 sec. In the same year he became the first man to break eight hours for the 52 mile London to Brighton walk, and in 1938 underlined his supremacy as the king of the road when he won the European 50 kilometres championship in Paris.

DAVID WILKIE
Great Britain (1953)

David Wilkie became Britain's first male Olympic swimming gold medallist for sixty-eight years in the 1976 Montreal Games when he won the 200 metres breaststroke in a world record 2 min 15.11 sec. He had pushed his great American rival John Hencken to a world record in the 100 metres when taking the silver medal but then reversed the positions with a magnificently judged finishing burst in his speciality event. David first revealed his tremendous potential as a member of the Warrender Baths Club in Edinburgh but it was not until he had taken a marine biology scholarship in Miami that he emerged as a world-beater. He made his Olympic debut in Munich in 1972, taking the silver medal in the 200 metres breaststroke behind Hencken, with whom he was to have a series of classic duels over the following four years. The Scot had a long, powerful stroke best suited to the longer of the two sprint events, and he won the world 200 metres breaststroke championship in 1973 and again in 1975, when he also captured the 100 metres title in the absence of Hencken. He is now building a career for himself as an ITV swimming commentator.

David Wilkie: a magnificently judged finish

PERCY WILLIAMS
Canada (1908-1983)

A nine-stone featherweight, Percy Williams was the lightest of all Olympic sprint champions when he pulled off a shock double in the 100 and 200 metres in the 1928 Amsterdam Games. He entered the Olympics as a twenty-year-old outsider but had been brought to a peak of perfection by his unorthodox but imaginative coach Bob Granger. When he returned home to his native Vancouver he was given a hero's welcome and a trust fund was set up to help him with his education and future training — this was more than half a century before trust funds were officially recognized for amateur athletes by the IAAF! In 1930 Williams became the first man to have a 10.3 sec 100 metres accepted as a world record. The following month he won the first British Empire Games 100 yards in 9.9 sec despite pulling a thigh muscle twenty-five yards from the tape. He was never the same force following the injury and made an impact only in the sprint relay in the 1932 Olympics when his pace helped Canada finish in fourth place.

HANS GUNTER WINKLER
West Germany (1926)

The son of a horse dealer from Westphalia, Hans Gunter Winkler could ride almost before he could walk, and in a career covering six Olympiads set an equestrianism record that will be difficult for anybody to equal. He won five Grand Prix gold medals — four team, one individual — plus a silver and a bronze. He had a memorable partnership with a former race-horse called Halla. Together they won the world championship in 1954 and 1955, and then the following year captured the individual Olympic title and led West Germany to the team gold. Winkler's triumph in the Melbourne Games was as much about courage as brilliant horsemanship. He tore a muscle in the first round and, despite being in acute agony, added two more clear rounds to clinch his victory. Winkler, still a master and extremely competitive at the age of fifty, looked set to collect a sixth gold medal in the 1976 Montreal Olympics but Alwin Schockemohle — his successor as the show-jumping king — had two fences down in the final round, thus dropping defending team champions West Germany into second place.

ARTHUR WINT
Jamaica (1920)

It was while serving as a pilot in the RAF during the Second World War that Arthur Wint started to fulfil the promise he had shown when as a raw eighteen-year-old he had won the 800 metres and come third in the 400 metres hurdles in the Central American Games. Standing 6ft 4in and with a stride close to ten feet, he was one of three magnificent athletes who brought Olympic glory to Jamaica in the immediate post-war years. He came a close second to Mal Whitfield in the 800 metres in 1948 and again in 1952 and ran a beautifully judged race to pip his talented team-mate Herb McKenley for the gold medal in the 400 metres in the London Games. Wint had seized up with cramp while running the third leg of the 4 x 400 metres relay in London and always felt guilty that he had let the Jamaican team down. He made full amends in Helsinki four years later when he gave them a 46.8 sec send-off on the first leg, with his team-mates Les Laing, Herb McKenley and 1952 individual champion George Rhoden stylishly finishing off what he had started to lift Jamaica to a thrilling victory over the United States in a world record 3 min 3.9 sec. Wint (who qualified in London as a doctor) was one of the most popular performers on British tracks for more than ten years.

BARBEL WOCKEL
East Germany (1955)

As Barbel Eckert, she caused one of the major upsets of the 1976 Montreal Olympics when — after scraping into the East German team as a third-string — she won the 200 metres in an Olympic record 22.37 sec. She again displayed her competitive qualities in the sprint relay when she made up lost ground on West Germany's 100 metres specialist Annegret Richter to anchor her team to victory in an Olympic record 42.55 sec. Four years later — after marriage and motherhood — Barbel repeated her double-gold performance in the Moscow Games, speeding to victory in the 200 metres in 22.03 sec from the tight inside lane and running the second leg for an East German team that produced a world record 41.60 sec in the sprint relay. A student of psychology, she was a hurdler before switching to the sprints and became a triple gold medallist in the junior European championships in 1973. Barbel, the first Olympic champion to retain a 200 metres title, was always able to 'psych' herself into peak form for the Olympic challenge following indifferent form in the interval years. She shares the women's four-gold Olympic record with Fanny Blankers-Koen and Betty Cuthbert, and hopes to overtake them in Los Angeles.

MAMO WOLDE
Ethiopia (1932)

Spectators at the 1956 Melbourne Games who saw Mamo Wolde finish last in his 800 metres heat, last in his 1500 metres heat and running the third leg for an Ethiopian relay team that finished last in its heat, could hardly have imagined that they were watching a future Olympic champion. Wolde refused to become disheartened and experimented with his running until he discovered that he was best suited to the distance events. He reappeared on the Olympic stage in Tokyo in 1964 and took a creditable fourth place in the 10,000 metres, but then dropped out of a marathon won for a second successive time by his compatriot Abebe Bikila. Four years later Wolde made the most of a life lived at high altitude when in Mexico's thin air he battled to a silver medal in the 10,000 metres and then ran a beautifully judged marathon to win by more than three minutes. He was back in action at the age of forty in the Munich Olympics and was always prominent in the marathon, finishing in third place to bring a satisfactory end to an Olympic career that was to say the least eventful.

DAVE WOTTLE
United States (1950)

Dave Wottle used to give coaches heart-failure with his unorthodox tactical running over the 800 metres course but the fact that he had a gold medal to show for his efforts in the 1972 Munich Olympics is proof positive that he knew just what he was doing. Wottle was an eccentric, likeable character who always stood out in a race because of the peaked golf cap that he used to wear. When he entered the US Olympic trials his personal best for 800 metres was 1 min 47.3 sec. He won the trials in a world-record-equalling 1 min 44.3 sec, got married the following week and then left with his bride for a European honeymoon after cheerfully telling the US team officials that he would see them in Munich! His final preparations for the Olympics were handicapped by an Achilles tendon injury and he seemed almost to gamble with getting a place in the final by running each of his preliminary races as a back marker and then coming through off the final bend to qualify. He had the cheek and the steel nerve to follow the same tactics in the final, suddenly sprinting from the back of the field to pip stumbling Russian Evgeni Arzhanov by a mere 3/100th of a second. There has never been an Olympic champion quite like him.

MIRUTS YIFTER
Ethiopia (c. 1944)

Tiny, bald-headed Miruts Yifter was following in some famous footsteps when he pulled off the 5000/10,000 metres track double in the 1980 Moscow Olympics. Hannes Kolehmainen, Paavo Nurmi, Emil Zatopek, Vladimir Kuts and Lasse Viren had been there before him, but none of these Olympic immortals could match his extraordinary background. Nicknamed 'Yifter the Shifter' because of his devastating finishing burst, Yifter is a father of six children who does not know just how old he is. He reckoned he was 'about thirty-eight' when he competed in Moscow but his official entry form had him down as born in 1947 and that was later amended to 1944! An officer in the Ethiopian air force, he first appeared in Olympic competition in 1972 when he finished third in the 10,000 metres and missed the 5000 metres final because he was in the toilet when the runners came

under starter's orders! The African boycott put him out of the 1976 Montreal Olympics when he was reckoned to be at his peak but he went to Moscow with three African championships and four World Cup victories to boost his confidence. The popular little Ethiopian — who always wins the hearts of the crowds — produced his famous finishing kick on cue in both the 5000 and 10,000 metres finals to take the gold medals in convincing style. He left the Olympic stage with the parting shot that he might be tempted to compete in the marathon in 1984, at which time his age could be anything between forty and forty-four.

EMIL ZATOPEK
Czechoslovakia (1922)

We have to come down among the Z-men to find perhaps the greatest of all Olympic heroes — Emil Zatopek, the legendary Czechoslovak track-master. He first stepped on to the Olympic stage in London in 1948 and made an immediate impact by winning the 10,000 metres, teasing and tormenting his rivals with sudden injections of pace that were to become so familiar to athletics followers over the next decade. Always appearing in agony because of the tortured, grimacing looks on his face, Emil went for the double in the 5000 metres but seemed to have surrendered the race to brilliant Belgian Gaston Reiff. He was fifty metres behind at the bell and then produced one of the most spectacular finishing sprints in Olympics history as he chopped Reiff's lead down to just one metre at the tape. Coaches scratched their heads as they watched Zatopek's eccentric tactics and wondered just what he would come up with in the future. Here obviously was a talent still in early bloom.

Zatopek had not started running seriously until he was almost forced to take part in a race at the age of eighteen while working in a local shoe factory in his home town of Koprivnice. He surprised himself by finishing second and started an instant love affair with athletics. His early progress was slow until he introduced 'interval' running into his training programme, mixing long jogging journeys with sudden bursts of speed — tactics with which he was to destroy a procession of rivals during his remarkable career. He established himself as an international-class runner in 1944 when in quick succession he broke the Czech records for 2000, 3000 and 5000 metres. When he was called up into the army in 1945 he increased his training output and ran daily distances of up to fifteen miles, often while wearing his heavy army boots. He got his first taste of world-class opposition in the 1946 European Games in Oslo, finishing fifth in the 5000 metres behind British hero Sydney Wooderson. The experience sharpened Zatopek's appetite and he returned home to Czechoslovakia to pour still more training miles into his preparation for what was to become Olympic immortality. In 1949 he set the first two of his eighteen world records, twice lowering the 10,000

Emil Zatopek: leads Chris Chataway in the 1952 5000 metres final

to Czechoslovakia to pour still more training miles into his preparation for what was to become Olympic immortality. In 1949 he set the first two of his eighteen world records, twice lowering the 10,000 metres mark. Over the next six years he created new records for distances from 5000 to 30,000 metres. No other athlete has ever been able to match this record output.

In the 1950 European championships he lapped every other runner to win the 10,000 metres by more than a minute and in the 5000 metres his winning margin was twenty-three seconds. During his final build-up to the 1952 Olympics he trailed in third behind two Russians in a 5000 metres race and the buzz went round the athletics world that he had burnt himself out. This conjecture was made to seem absurd in Helsinki when Zatopek achieved the greatest treble triumph in Olympic history — the 5000 metres and 10,000 metres in Olympic record times and then, incredibly, the marathon in his first attempt at the distance, winning by more than two minutes. His wife Dana — born on exactly the same day as Emil, September 19, 1922 — completed a unique family double in Helsinki when she won the gold medal in the women's javelin event. The amazing Zatopek returned to his beloved Olympic arena for a farewell run in 1956 when, just a matter of

Opposite **Miruts Yifter: shifted into top gear in Moscow**

weeks after a hernia operation, he finished sixth in the marathon which was won by his old friend and rival Alain Mimoun. He fell foul of the political hierarchy in Czechoslovakia in the late 1960s after identifying with the freedom fighters and was stripped of many of the privileges he had earned as the world's most renowned athlete but nobody could ever take away his premier spot as an Olympic hero for all seasons.

LEONID ZHABOTINSKY
USSR (1938)

'The Great Zhabo' started his weight-lifting career at the age of fifteen and within ten years had established himself as an awe-inspiring strongman of his sport. He dethroned his previously unbeaten countryman Yuri Vlasov in the 1964 Tokyo Olympics, producing a world record jerk on his last attempt to clinch the gold medal. Standing 6ft 6in and weighing more than twenty-five stone, Zhabo was the undisputed king of the 'iron game' over the next five years and retained his Olympic crown in Mexico in 1968 with a total lift of 1262 lb — identical to his record lift in the 1964 Games. Zhabo, a colourful character who captured world-wide interest with his expressive approach to weight-lifting, inexplicably retired in mid-contest when defending his world title in 1969 and was never seen on the international platform again.

143

BRENDAN FOSTER'S

OLYMPIC
HEROES
1896 - 1984

PAST OLYMPIC CHAMPIONS AND THE FAVOURITES FOR L.A. '84

BRENDAN FOSTER'S

OLYMPIC
HEROES
1896 - 1984

PAST OLYMPIC CHAMPIONS AND THE FAVOURITES FOR L.A.'84

HARRAP   LONDON

First published in Great Britain 1984
by HARRAP LIMITED
19-23 Ludgate Hill, London EC4M 7PD

ISBN 0 245-54200-0

All photographs are reproduced by courtesy
of All-Sport Photographic Limited

Designed by Michael R. Carter

Printed and bound in Great Britain
by R. J. Acford, Chichester